Amartya Sen's Hindu Bash

About the author

V. S. Sardesai, B. Sc. (Hons.), LL.M. (Advocate), was born at Panaji (Goa) in 1935 and shifted to Mumbai in 1952 for higher studies. After working in legal departments of various institutions, he retired as Asst. General Manager (Law) from Bank of India in 1993 and thereafter worked as Legal Consultant in Indian Institute of Bankers (IIB) and Bank of Tokyo–Mitsubishi till he shifted to Bangalore in Oct. 2004. His articles on legal matters were published in several legal magazines as also in newspapers such as *Financial Express*. Because of his special interest in religion, philosophy and history he has written articles on historical subjects, which are published in leading magazines.

Amartya Sen's Hindu Bash

V.S. Sardesai

Readworthy
New Delhi

First published 2008

Published and printed by
Readworthy Publications Pvt. Ltd.
A-18, Mohan Garden
Near Nawada Metro Station
New Delhi – 110 059 (India)
Phone: 011 2537 1324 Fax: +91 11 2537 1323
Email: info@readworthypub.com
Web: www.readworthypub.com

Cataloging in Publication Data — DK
Courtesy: D.K. Agencies (P) Ltd. <docinfo@dkagencies.com>

Sardesai, V.S. (Vasant Sidbarao), 1935-
Amartya Sen's Hindu bash / V.S. Sardesai.
ix, 102 p. 22 cm.
Amartya Sen, b. 1933, Indian economist.
Includes bibliographical references (p.)
Includes index.

ISBN 13: 978-81-89973-08-7 (PB) ISBN 10: 81-89973-08-8

1. Sen, Amartya, 1933- --Religion. 2. Hindutva. 3. Hinduism and politics--India. 4. Civilization, Hindu. 5. Indus civilization. 6. Indo-Aryans--Origin. 7. India--History--To 324 BC. I. Title.

DDC 294.509 54 22

Preface

It is said that a scholar should always be a student. In Hindu tradition a student is not supposed to accept any teaching even if it is given by Brahma himself unless he himself is satisfied and has experienced the truth behind it. No doubt one should have faith in one's guru. But it should not be blind faith. Faith begins where logic ends. It is not against logic but beyond it. At present, most of us are having blind faith in what is being said by the so-called experts without verifying the truth behind it even though what is said by such experts may be against logic, and we formulate our ideas and opinions based on such experts. It is said of a Zen Master that one day he was pouring tea in a cup when a renowned professor came to see him and requested him to teach Zen. The Master did not say anything but continued pouring the tea in the cup even though it was full and overflowing.

The professor could not help remarking that when the cup is full what is the use in pouring tea in the same cup. Therupon the Master said that if you want to have tea, your cup should be empty. For studying Zen, you should have an empty mind. You should not have any preconceived notions or perceptions about Zen.

Nowadays it has become a norm or fashion to criticize, abuse, distort, denigrate and ridicule Hinduism and Hindus as if they have got no defenders. Amartya Sen's *The*

Argumentative Indian is a book, which is full of such prejudice and bias against Hinduism and Hindus. From reading his book, it appears that he is allergic to the words Hinduism and Hindus. When a learned man of the calibre of Amartya Sen writes such a book, he should have taken more care and should have been impartial and verified both the sides especially while writing on Hinduism and Hindus. It is said that when a person gets converted to another religion, he becomes more orthodox than the persons already following that religion — "more Christian than Christ". I can understand Britishers targeting Hinduism for obvious reasons and to help the missionaries. But it becomes disgusting and disturbing when we, Indians, follow them without verifying the truth relying on their so-called researches and inventions, even though it appears illogical on the face of it especially when there are researches made not only by Indians but also by Westerners pointing out and showing the correct facts. Unfortunately in India, we have renowned but committed historians who are wedded to some ideology or philosophy rather than to history as a result history often becomes a casualty. Historical data and facts are twisted, misinterpreted and distorted to suit and bring them in conformity with their ideology, which has become defunct. New researches and the facts that are brought to light and which contradict their ideology or their findings and opinions are ignored or suppressed.

When I read both his books *The Argumentative Indian* and *Identity and Violence*, I was greatly disturbed and shocked because Hinduism, which is already being denigrated and distorted for obvious reasons and which is being wiped out slowly because of the behaviour and actions of the so-called pseudo-seculars and our narrow-minded politicians for their petty interest, is shown in poor light on the basis of the writings of such committed historians whose main object and interest in history appears to be to support their ideology even by raping it rather than to find out the truth. Mr Sen should have impartially examined all the proofs available before writing the books. Instead, he blindly followed these Hindu-baiter historians.

In my book I have attempted to point out the truth by highlighting the discrepancies and paradoxes, which have cropped up because of accepting these theories such as the Aryan invasion of India, that Sri Rama was a myth and *Ramayana* is a parable, that the description of the mighty Saraswati in the *Rig Veda* is in fact description of a river from outside India etc. and to show that these paradoxes have cropped up only because of and after our accepting these theories as gospel truth.

And the more we try to justify these findings, it gives rise to further paradoxes. My purpose in writing the book is more to bring out the truth than to criticize his books. I am aware that my role in this attempt to remove the misconceptions and misunderstandings about Hinduism and Vedas is even less than the role of the squirrel in building the Ram Setu. But I have done it because of my conviction that it is the duty of every Hindu, if not Indian, to accept something only after verifying the facts and convinced about its truth and not because somebody says so. How far I am successful in the attempt, only the readers will know.

I take the opportunity to thank the publishers Readworthy Publications Pvt. Ltd. and Shri Surya P. Mittal for agreeing to publish the book on such a dry subject.

V.S. Sardesai

in memory of

my best friend Babubhai, *alias*

Late Harshavardhan G. Vakil

and

brother-in-Law Gurubhau, *alias*

Late Manguesh S. Mahatme

but for whom I would not have been what I am

Contents

1

Are not Buddhism and Jainism off-shoots of Sanatana Dharma?

AMARTYA SEN, Nobel Laureate told Dabashish Mukerji (CELEBTALK, *The Week*, 11 September, 2005): "I think the main threat to secularism in India comes from Hindutva. I don't think radical Islam has much to do with it. Hindutva exponents have not been saying, "Muslims are getting radicalized, so should we." I think the Hindutva movement targets not so much radical Islam, as the secularist position of the Congress and the Left. The Hindutvaites' argument is that Indian secularists, or what they call pseudo-secularists, overlook the nastiness of Muslim rulers of India. That is not the reaction to radical Islam at all."

Before commenting on his above observation, I would like to refer to and discuss the third chapter "India: Large and Small" of Part one of his recently published book *The Argumentative Indian* (Allen Lane — an imprint of Penguin Books, 2005) wherein even though he has attacked Hindutva and not Hinduism as such along with BJP and Sangh Parivar, in fact, most of the events and the grounds taken by him are the same as taken by other Hindu baiters for attacking Hindus and Hinduism and which have been replied time and again by different persons. It is the same old wine in a new bottle. The only reason for repeating the same thing again and again by different persons appears to be in line with the age-old practice of repeating the same thing over and again till people start believing the same. There is also a Russian proverb that if you want to kill a dog, call it mad. Before starting, I would like to make it clear that I am neither a member of BJP nor of Sangh Parivar nor have I taken any brief on their behalf. I am however a Hindu and am proud to call myself a Hindu and of my Hindutva.

Mr Sen says that he does not want to enter into the difficult question of the role Hindu tradition may have played in sustaining a dialogic culture and the tolerance of heterodoxy in India, and that some of the most articulate and ardent advocates of tolerance and mutual respect in India were not themselves Hindus, such as Ashoka, who was a Buddhist and Akbar who was a Muslim, but they too belonged to a broad culture in which Hindu heterodoxy was vigorously present. He asserts that in fact Buddhism is arguably as much an inheritor of the earlier Indian traditions of Vedas and the Upanishads as Hinduism is, since both the religious traditions drew on these classics. Scholars in China, Japan and other countries were introduced to the Upanishads mainly through the studies of Buddhism.

From the above, it is clear that Mr Sen wants us to believe or wants to create an impression that Buddhism and Jainism are parallel to Hinduism coming from the same source, whose religious traditions are drawn from or based on Vedas and Upanishads which is factually incorrect, as both Buddhism and Jainism have come from Hinduism which was known as Sanatana Dharma at that time. At the time of Buddha or Mahavira who was the founder of Jainism, there was nothing like Hinduism in India. There was Sanatana Dharma, which was followed by everyone including both Buddha and Mahavira. Hinduism is the name given to Sanatana Dharma subsequently. Sanatana Dharma is a very broad based Dharma. In fact, it cannot be called a *dharma* in the restricted sense the term *dharma* or religion is understood like Christianity or Islam. It never asked its followers or insisted that its followers should pray or follow a particular Godhead or Prophet, as is the case with Christianity or Islam. In that sense it may be called a sort of amalgam of religions or world religion. So also it believed that for spiritual solace or advancement, there are as many paths as there are individuals and each one can follow the path one feels proper for one's advancement. It is not dogmatic like Christianity or Islam that insists that for one's salvation one should pray and follow only a particular God or Prophet, for otherwise such a person will not only not get the salvation but on the other hand will go permanently to a hell. As Buddha and Mahavira could not get satisfaction in following the path that was followed by common people at that time they searched for their own path as per the tradition and when they got the spiritual solace by following their path they started preaching it and thus Buddhism and Jainism were born and their followers were called as Buddhists and Jains respectively. Recently when Jains applied to the Supreme Court to treat them as a minority religion and not as a part of Hindu community, in order to get the benefits given to the minority communities under the Indian Constitution, the Supreme Court ruled that the Constitution of India does not view Sikhs and Jains as separate national minorities beyond the periphery of Hindu religion. Since both Buddha and Mahavira were the followers of Sanatana Dharma, which is based on Vedas and Upanishads, naturally both Buddhism and Jainism follow the religious tradition drawn on Vedas and Upanishads.

As regards his statement about the role Hindu tradition may have played in sustaining a dialogic culture and tolerance of heterodoxy or that both Ashoka and Akbar belonged to a broad culture in which Hindu heterodoxy was vigorously present, it is rather mischievous. It should be noted that there is no question of Hindu tradition playing a role in sustaining a dialogic culture or Hindu heterodoxy being vigorously present therein, for there is nothing like a separate Indian culture which is different from Hindu culture and right from the beginning it was Hindu culture and the Hindu culture only from time immemorial, and the contentions of some that Aryans or Hindus were subsequent inhabitants of India is a myth spread for some purpose or with ulterior motives which shall be discussed later. As such the question of Hindu tradition playing a role in sustaining Indian culture does not arise. It can be said in respect of other cultures such as Islam and Christianity, which have come subsequently, and the role played by them, if any, in influencing and sustaining our culture. Our culture is fully based on Hindu tradition. Otherwise all other communities who have come to India such as Parsees, Khojas, Muslims, Christians, Jews and others who have made India their home would have never been welcomed and helped to establish their religious places in India even before they invaded India. Since it is the Hindu culture right from the beginning, how can the question of separate contribution of Hindu tradition or Hindu heterodoxy to the culture of India arise? The question of role played by other religions such as Christianity and Islam in sustaining a dialogic culture of India and tolerance of heterodoxy, I am afraid it is negative and I have discussed the same in detail in my recently published book *Can a Secular be a Fundamentalist*? How can dogmatic religions which cannot tolerate other religions and are bent upon finishing other religions by either converting their followers and bringing them into their fold or otherwise even by killing them, be called tolerant or contribute to a broad based culture like Hindu culture? As regards Ashoka, he was a Hindu king before he adopted Buddhism and in any case his culture was Hindu culture. As regards Akbar, he wanted to form a new religion by adopting all good things from all religions. Naturally he wanted to adopt tolerance and heterodoxy from Sanatana Dharma in his new religion. As mentioned above Sanatana Dharma is a very broad-based religion if at all it can be called a religion, and hence Hindu culture is naturally a dialogic and broad-based culture.

2

Is not Ayodhya Rama's Birthplace?

AMARTYA SEN further alleges that many political activists nowadays are bent on doing away with the broad and tolerant parts of the Hindu tradition in favour of a uniquely ascertained view, which, they demand, must be accepted, and gives an example to show how earlier Hindu tradition was broad-based and tolerant by referring to the discussion between Rama and Javali in *Ramayana,* where Javali describes the decision taken by Rama as extremely foolish. He, however, does not give any reason for his assertion that nowadays the political activists are bent on doing away with the broad and tolerant parts of the Hindu tradition; maybe because of the prejudice he bears against Hinduism or because of the soft corner he has for minority religions. I, however, propose to discuss the reasons why nowadays many political activists are bent on doing away with the broad and tolerant part of the Hindu tradition as alleged by him after commenting on his allegations on Sri Rama and Babri Masjid.

Mr Sen emphasizes that he is the same Rama whose divinity has been an act of faith in recently politicized Hinduism. I do not understand the purpose of Mr Sen emphasizing that he is the *same* Rama. Does he want to show that earlier the Hindus were tolerant to criticism but now they are not so? If so, he should give proof for his allegations. Or does he want to signify that because Javali criticizes Rama's act, he (Rama) cannot be divine and we should not have any faith in his divinity? Or that if he were divine, his act would not have been criticized? Mr Sen has himself admitted that Hinduism is a broad-based and tolerant religion. If so, why did he emphasize that he is the *same* Rama? Our faith in the divinity of our gods is not so weak and shaky that if someone criticizes our gods we will give up the faith. Recently in Benni Hinn's grand show in Bangalore, papers and circulars were distributed denigrating and abusing Hindu gods. It does not mean that Hindus should lose faith in their gods if someone criticizes or abuses their gods. It only shows the meanness of the persons abusing. It is only the minority religious communities that cannot tolerate even an honest criticism of their gods or Prophets. They treat it as blasphemy.

Now let us consider the example given by him as a proof of his allegation that nowadays many Hindu political activists are bent on doing away with the broad and tolerant part of the Hindu tradition. He says that these political Hindu activists consider Sri Rama as an incarnation of god and claim that all Hindus worship him and that he was born on a well identified spot nine lakh years ago. Mr Sen's further statement is rather puzzling. He says that he and persons like him are thus not allowed to see the *Ramayana* as "a marvellous parable" (as Rabindranath Tagore saw it) but as a historical document, which cannot be questioned. I do not understand how is he prevented or not allowed to see *Ramayana* as "a marvellous parable" only because these political activists consider Sri Rama as an incarnation of god? Only because some persons hold one view does it mean that others are prevented from holding any other view? Or is it that because Sen and the like-minded persons feel that *Ramayana* is "a marvellous parable," he wants all others also to hold the same view and if someone differs, he feels that he is not allowed to hold his views? Or is it because Rabindranath Tagore also holds the same view that *Ramayana* is "a marvellous parable" he wants everyone to see *Ramayana* as a parable? For his information, not only Hindu political activists but also many Hindus like me look upon *Ramayana* as a historical document and Rama as a historical person. Not only that; we feel that *Ramayana* and *Mahabharata* are our cultural heritage. Many places in India are connected with *Ramayana* and *Mahabharata*. And we feel that every Indian — not only Hindus — should be proud of the same and should try to preserve the same. Otherwise, he is unfit to be called an Indian. However, we do not and, in any case, cannot prevent others from holding any other view. And only because one holds the view that *Ramayana* is a historical document, one cannot be considered as doing away with the broad and tolerant part of the Hindu tradition as alleged by Mr Sen.

Regarding marvellous parable, the Christian missionaries, while propagating Christianity and converting Hindus to their fold used to say to Hindus that their gods are from the parables and not historical but Christ was a historical personality who had actually lived in this world even though they had no documentary proof to support their claim. However they got their first jolt when what is now called Dead Sea Scroll was discovered in 1947. And after initial publication, when the Church authorities found it embarrassing, instead of publishing it fully for the sake of truth, they managed to suppress its publication for about 50 years when someone managed to get copies of the same and published it with the result that now there is a serious question mark whether Christ was a historical personality or only a myth.

Mr Sen challenges the claim of the Hindus that the Babri Masjid stood, before its demolition, precisely at the site of an earlier Hindu temple, destroyed by Babur to build the mosque. He further says that the historical claim has to be distinguished from the more gigantic claim that Rama, the divine incarnation, was born there, before recorded history began. Having raised the topic it will not be proper to leave it half way as Mr Sen has done as it creates a wrong impression resulting in drawing wrong inferences. In fact, I have dealt with the subject in my book *Can a Secular be a Fundamentalist*? recently published by Hindu Voice. But since he has raised the topic, I shall deal with the same in a nutshell. But before giving the facts I shall discuss his comments that the historical claim has to be distinguished from the more gigantic claim that Rama was born there before the recorded history began. I do not understand what he meant by "before the recorded history began." For Hindus like me *Ramayana* itself is a recorded history. Is there anything separate like recorded history? Is there any procedure to have historical facts recorded? And as per Mr Sen when did the recorded history begin? I have found that eminent historians have challenged even the facts recorded by persons accompanying Mahmud Ghazni on the ground that there are exaggerations. And if there is no recorded history, are we supposed to deny the existence of the facts? Even in Christianity when a serious doubt was raised whether Christ was a historical figure or a myth, they are now saying that it is their faith in Christ. So also even though Christ's birth is celebrated all over the world on 25 December, he was not born on that date and it is only because of the faith that it is celebrated on that day. If so, can't the Hindus say that it is their faith that Rama was born there as recorded in the *Ramayana*, which for them, is also a historical record? And how can the historical facts be distinguished and differ from the claim that Sri Rama was born there if otherwise it can be proved that Sri Rama was born there? Only because the Hindus feel that Sri Rama was a divine incarnation and Mr Sen feels that his birth was before the beginning of recorded history, the historical claim should be distinguished from the claim that Sri Rama was born there? There are of course other historical data, which I shall discuss presently to show that there are reasons to believe that Rama was born there. But let us first see the facts about the so-called Babri Masjid or mosque.

One Mir Baqi constructed it on the orders of Babur in 1528 after destruction and demolition of the then existing Rama temple at a place in Ayodhya known as Janmabhoomi adjacent to what is known as Sita-ki-Rasoi, Sita being the wife of Rama. The Masjid was known as Masjid-i-Janmastan or Masjid-i-Sita-ki-Rasoi till recently up to 1989. It was also an accepted truth that the Masjid was constructed after destroying the then existing temple under Babur's orders as was the practice of these barbarian looters and invaders to destroy the temples and to build Masjids in their places, in many cases by utilizing the materials of the temples. Up to 1989 everyone accepted the fact that the Masjid was built after destroying the then existing Rama's temple. Even 1989 edition of *Encyclopedia Britannica* (entry Ayodhya) confirms the temple destruction scenario. However, after 1989 all of a sudden Muslims started arguing that Babur did not order the destruction of the temple for construction of the mosque, without giving any evidence for their statement. On the other hand, they asked Hindus to produce evidence that there was an existing temple, which was destroyed by Babur for the construction of the mosque, even though, it is for the party challenging the accepted facts to produce the evidence to prove its claim, if it wants to challenge the facts accepted from time immemorial. And as such the claim of the Muslims that there was no temple, which was destroyed by Babur for construction of the mosque, cannot be considered, unless they support it by proper evidence. Further since 1936 no Namaz was offered from that place, as in a court case the Muslims had agreed not to use the Masjid for offering Namaz and since 1949 Hindus were using it for prayers. So even though it was a Muslim Masjid, since 1936 the Muslims did not use it as a mosque while Hindus were using the place for offering prayers. These being the facts, now let us consider the reasons for, in the words of Mr Sen, the more gigantic claim of Hindu political activists that Rama, the divine incarnation, was born there, before recorded history began. I do not know when as per Mr Sen the recorded history has begun. But the reasons for considering that Sri Rama was born there are as under:

1. From time immemorial the place was known as the birthplace of Sri Rama. It is not that these Hindu political activists for the first time put up the claim that Sri Rama was born there. As stated above the place was known as Rama's Janmabhoomi or Janmasthan even before the construction of the mosque by Mir Baqi. Not only that, but even after construction of the mosque, it came to be known as Masjid-i-Janmasthan or Masjid-i-Sita-ki-Rasoi. And it can neither be the Janmastan of Babur nor of Mir Baqi. Moreover Sita being the wife of Sri Rama, her Rasoi can only be adjacent to Sri Rama's Janmabhoomi or Janmasthan.
2. From recent archaeological excavation report, it is clear that the Masjid was built on the place where there existed a temple.
3. *Encyclopedia Britannica* (1989 edition) confirms the existence of Rama temple before the construction of the mosque.
4. Ancient Sanskrit text of Ayodhya Mahatmya of *Skanda Purana* composed centuries before the invasion of Babur confirms the existence of Janmasthan temple in the Ramkot.

5. Joseph Tieffenthater (1710-85), a Jesuit priest of Austrian origin says that the fortress called Ramkot was destroyed where a Mohammedan temple with three domes was built up.
6. Mirza Jan in *Hadiqah-i-Shuhada* in 1856 says that the invaders cleared up Faizabad and Auadh because it was a great centre of worship and capital of Rama's father where there stood the great temple, there they built a big mosque. The Janmasthan temple is the principal place of Rama's incarnation, adjacent to which is Sita-ki-Rasoi. Hence king Babur built a lofty mosque up there and the mosque is still known as Masjid-i-Sita-ki-Rasoi.
7. *Ramayana* which for Hindus like me is a history even though Mr Sen and his tribe considers it as only "a marvellous parable", clearly says Ayodhya is the birthplace of Sri Rama.

I however agree with Mr Sen that it does not give a licence for religious vandalism or sectarian destruction or to tear down a place of worship of other people and there is no justification for the demolition of Babri Masjid in 1992. At the same time we should not forget about the dangerous trend that has cropped up recently and that is to take the law into one's own hands instead of following the due procedure of law. Leave aside the destruction of Babri Masjid, but nowadays the tendency of some financial institutions, whenever there is a default committed by the borrowers especially in car loans, is to appoint a recovery agency who instead of taking legal actions against such borrowers for recovery of dues, forcibly take possession of the vehicles from such borrowers and recover the dues by selling the vehicles. So also even the individual in order to recover his dues from others many a time take help of gangsters instead of going for legal actions. Not only that, but when it was found that the crimes in Mumbai were going out of control, and there were encounter killings by the police, it came down substantially. And what is the reason? Why nowadays there is this tendency developed to take the law into one's own hand? It is said that justice delayed is justice denied. How much time it takes to get justice in India? One cannot get the judgement even in a couple of years. It takes decades. In case of Babri Masjid even after about 50 years, the matter did not come up for final hearing before the demolition. Not only that but even after demolition now more than a decade has passed, but we are yet to get the judgement. Similar is the case in recovering the financial institutions' dues or the dues of the individuals. In case of criminals, they are not afraid of the law because many a time the criminal dies even before he is chargesheeted. And in many cases he gets the benefit of doubt. Only when there were encounter deaths the crimes in Mumbai came down. It is not that the government is not aware of the situation. In order to ease the situation it has taken some round-about steps such as Consumer Forums and Lok-Adalats. But in Lok-Adalats it is the bank that suffers since generally the bank is asked as to how much sacrifice it is ready to make and the bank agrees since otherwise it has to wait for a very long period to recover its dues. But ultimately the defendant is benefited. Unless a permanent solution is found out immediately to get the justice within a reasonable time, the situation is bound to go out of hand.

I shall now consider the reasons why many Hindu political activists nowadays seem bent on doing away with the broad and tolerant part of the Hindu tradition as alleged by Mr Sen.

3

Indian Secularism-Minorityism

Now let us see the reasons, if any, why many Hindu political activists nowadays, as alleged by Mr Amartya Sen, seem bent on doing away with the broad and tolerant parts of the Hindu tradition of liberty and tolerance, the tradition of elaborate presentation of alternate points of view and of accommodating heterodoxy. Mr Sen further alleges that in addition to favouring narrowly religious certainty, these Hindu political activists prefer to dwell on interreligious confrontations, rather than on the tradition of the peaceful presence of different faiths side by side. He says that a continuation of the tolerant and receptive tradition can also be found in the writings of leaders such as Gandhi or Tagore. I fully agree with Mr Sen that the Hindu tradition is broad and tolerant. The question is why, if at all, many Hindu political activists are now bent on doing away with the broad and tolerant part of the Hindu tradition? Are they deriving any advantage by favouring such narrowly religious certainty? On the other hand, they are accused and charged for breaking the age-old broad and tolerant Hindu tradition. Or as questioned by Mr Sen, is it because "Muslims are getting radicalized, so should we" even though they are not saying so? But what do we mean by a radical or fundamentalist? A person who follows the religion strictly both in spirit and in words. For Muslims, the fundamental principle of their religion Islam is to convert the whole world into Islam. A duty is cast on them under their religion to convert others to their religion or to kill them. Not only in Islam but also in Christianity such a duty is cast on their followers. They are intolerant to other religions. They cannot tolerate any other religion except their own and that is why there were religious wars between them, crusades, *jihad*s and inquisitions when billions of innocent people were killed. In any case what the Muslims and Christians have done or are doing is in fulfilment of their religious duty. Can the same thing be said about the Hindus? Is such a duty cast on the followers of Hinduism? On the other hand, Hinduism is broad and tolerant to others whatever may be their religion, caste or creed. If Hindus become radicals or fundamentalists, naturally they will be more tolerant and broad as per the Hindu tradition. So how can a Hindu be a radical and at the same time intolerant? Will it not be contradictory?

Before answering the question and discussing the reasons why many Hindu political activists are bent on doing away with the broad and tolerant part of the Hindu tradition, let us examine his statement that a continuation of the tolerant and receptive tradition can be found in the writings of leaders such as Mahatma Gandhi and Tagore *vis-à-vis* their behaviour under certain circumstances. I do not know whether Mr Sen is aware of the advice given by Mahatma Gandhi to Christian missionaries who were engaged in converting poor and illiterate Hindus especially Hindu tribals through the so-called social work of education and health care. He told them that if they can convince him that their religion is superior to Hinduism, then he would be the first one, to get converted to their religion. But if their ultimate aim and main purpose of establishing educational institutions and hospitals is to convert the poor and illiterate Hindus to their fold, they should better pack off and go back to their countries and we do not require such social work of theirs even at the cost of remaining poor and undeveloped. So also Tagore returned the knighthood as a protest for the killing by General Dyer in Jalianwalla Baug. What does this prove? Even Gandhiji and Tagore could not tolerate certain things though both of them were followers of Hinduism. In other words there is a certain limit for tolerance. If that limit is crossed, no one can remain tolerant. And in spite of this, if one remains tolerant, it cannot be called tolerance but cowardice. The question is whether that limit has been crossed or not. No doubt, Hindu tradition, which every Hindu is supposed to follow, is broad and tolerant. But if someone by taking undue advantage of the tolerance of the Hindus threatens the very existence of Hindus, no one can or should expect Hindus to remain tolerant till they are extinguished. It appears that Mr Sen has got some strange ideas about the tolerance in Hinduism. He feels that even if other minority religious communities commit atrocities against Hindus, abuse Hinduism and try their best to ensure that Hinduism is wiped off from our world by conversion or otherwise, still Hindus should remain tolerant because Hindu tradition is broad and tolerant. He forgets that it is the minority communities, viz. the Muslims and Christians, by taking undue advantage of the Hindu tradition of tolerance are converting poor and illiterate Dalits, tribals and persons of lower castes *en masse* into their folds in the guise of social work, of course with the help of the so-called seculars. If some Hindus object to the same, immediately these pseudo seculars and persons like Mr Sen accuse and charge them that they are doing away with the broad and tolerant Hindu tradition and brand them as communalists and fundamentalists. In fact, one of the reasons for the Hindutva movement is that it has started as a reaction to the activities of these minority communities of trying to convert Hindus to their religions as also to the behaviour of these pseudo-seculars in their dealings with Hindus as against Muslims and Christians. It seems that Mr Sen and other seculars want Hindus to remain tolerant till all the Hindus are wiped away from our earth. But they forget that if Hinduism gets extinguished and disappears, religious tolerance will also disappear with it for Christianity and Islam are neither tolerant nor secular irrespective of what these pseudo-seculars may claim, and if they appear to be tolerant or secular it is only for convenience and as a matter of policy for attaining their aim. Here I cannot resist the temptation of narrating a story, which was told to us in our childhood. There was a cobra living on the side of a road and whenever the people used to pass by that road he used to hiss with the result that people were scared while passing through that road. There was a school nearby and young students also had to pass through that road. One day a saint was passing by that road. The cobra as usual hissed at him. He advised the cobra not to scare the passersby by hissing. The cobra agreed and from that day he stopped hissing. When the students found that he has stopped hissing initially someone threw a stone at him but when they found that he has really stopped hissing even if stones are thrown on him, they started throwing stones at him and injuring him and his conditions became miserable. After some days the same saint was passing on that road. He saw the conditions of the cobra and enquired. When he came to know of the facts, he told the cobra that he has not advised him to be so tolerant as not to hiss even if someone attacks him. Instead of the saint, had there been Mr Sen or these pseudo-seculars, I am sure they would have congratulated the cobra and advised it to continue to remain tolerant till it dies. Instead of criticizing and attacking Hindus, had Mr Sen advised the religious minorities to be tolerant to other religions and stop their conversion activities, it would have really helped India in attaining national integration and to preserve the tradition of peaceful presence of different faiths side by side.

Mr Sen says that a secular democracy, which gives equal room to every citizen irrespective of religious background, cannot be fairly defined in terms of the majority religion of the country. He further says that there is a difference between a constitutionally secular nation with a majority Hindu population and a theocratic Hindu state that might see Hinduism as an official religion. But, no matter what the official standing of any community or a group may be, the status of an individual citizen cannot be compromised by the smallness of the group to which such individual belongs. And he cites the example of United States when it declared independence in 1776 in which the different religious communities were quite diverse in size even though the Christians were in majority. But US Constitution took a neutral view of the specific beliefs of the different communities including Christian community.

Here, the question is who is asking or insisting to define a secular democracy in terms of majority religion of the country? Surely not Hindus or even Hindu fundamentalists who, on the other hand, are insisting to have Common Civil Code (not the Hindu laws or Hindu Code as some of these pseudo-seculars propagate) for all Indian citizens irrespective of religion, caste or creed, and that words like majority and minority should be removed from the discourse because perceptions of community-based interest should be replaced by perceptions of a seamless national interest where community identity is superseded by and gives way to a larger national identity. On the other hand, it is the so-called seculars that brand the Hindus as communalists for holding such views. It is they who, while preaching for national integration, work for national disintegration, who speak of abolition of caste system, while encouraging castes and sub-castes. For their petty interest, they are dividing India on castes and sub-castes basis, on religious minority and majority basis and they want to keep it in perpetuity.

I fully agree with Mr Sen that a secular democracy cannot be fairly defined in terms of the majority or minority religion of the country. Secularism means non-interference of the religion in the affairs of the state. Mr Sen says that when in 1776 United States declared independence, in spite of having different religious communities, it did not derail the need for the US Constitution to take a neutral view of the specific beliefs of the members of the different communities including Christian community irrespective of group dimensions. He insists that the respective sizes of the different religious communities should not be allowed to disrupt the rights, including the sense of belonging that every citizen should be able to enjoy. But who had prevented the Indian leaders who were at the helm of affairs at the time of Independence from adopting analogous provisions in the Indian Constitution? Surely not Hindus. The US Constitution has not made any special provisions in their Constitution for the religious minority communities by giving them special rights in the garb of protecting their interest. When both the cases, Indian and US, were similar, where was the necessity to differentiate Indian secularism from other secularisms of the world? It seems that these pseudo-seculars do not agree that where there are two or more religions in a state, there can be only two types of democracies. One is a theocratic democracy where, even though it may be a democracy, the state is governed by the laws and rules of the majority religion like that of Pakistan or Bangladesh. The second is secular democracy where the state does not allow the interference of any religion irrespective whether it is a majority or minority religion, in its affairs. This is the form that is adopted by most of the Western democratic countries including USA and which should have been adopted by India. But our so-called secular democrats or secular fundamentalists have adopted and carved out a third type of democracy and that is what I term as minorityism. They have given special rights and privileges to the minorities under the Constitution, as also they have divided the common laws not into two categories, viz. civil and criminal, as is the case in other states, but into three by adding one more category, viz. personal without defining their boundaries. In fact, both civil and criminal laws are or can also be called personal laws in the sense that all laws are made to govern the individuals. Further they say that while civil and criminal laws are in the domain of the state, personal laws are in the domain of the religious communities, and where minority religious communities are concerned, state should not interfere with it unless such communities voluntarily request the state to pass the laws affecting their personal rights. But it appears that for such seculars, the same principle does not apply where the majority religious community is concerned. While scrupulously avoiding any interference in the so-called personal laws of the minority communities, such secular government with impunity interferes with similar personal laws of the majority community. Passing of various Hindu Acts during Nehru's period and the amendment to Hindu Succession Act passed recently are the examples of such interferences. Not only that, but taking over the management of Hindu temples and Mutts and appointing persons of other religious communities as trustees thereon surely cannot be considered as non-interference in the religious affairs of the majority community by such governments. But it appears that for these pseudo-seculars such acts of the governments are secular acts. Their secularism means non-interference in the religious and personal affairs of only the minority religious communities and not of the majority community. Nowadays the minority communities have even formed their own personal courts to decide on such personal matters, which I feel, is unconstitutional.

The second reason why I call what is being followed in India is not secularism but minorityism, is that while refusing to construct the famous Somanatha temple at government's cost and castigating the then government of Saurashtra for contributing Rs.500,000 as one-time donation, Pandit Nehru, the then prime minister of India and an apostle of secularism in the words of Shri Mani Shankar Aiyar, not only pressurized the then Home Minister Sardar Patel to repair and renovate the mosques in Delhi at government expense, but also got the Haj Act passed by the Parliament whereunder pilgrimage by Muslim pilgrims to Haj is heavily subsidized — the present cost of the subsidy is more than Rs.200 crore per year. In my recently published book *Can a Secular be a Fundamentalist*? I have explained in detail why I call the Indian secularism as minorityism in the garb of secularism.

Mr Sen has accused Hindu political activists of preferring to dwell on inter-religious confrontation, rather than on the tradition of the peaceful presence of different faiths side by side, without giving any proof or evidence for his accusation. He says that since the Hindutva movement has been accompanied by violent physical actions, including the killing and terrorizing of minorities (as happened in Mumbai in 1992-

93 and in Gujarat in 2002), it is difficult to have patience with the intellectual belief and public proclamations. I do not know whether before making such baseless allegations and accusations and speaking about patience, Mr Sen was aware of the facts that in more than 90 per cent cases of riots, the minorities especially the Muslims are responsible for starting riots against Hindus and that the main cause for starting riots in Gujarat in 2002 was the horrid act of Muslims in roasting alive the Hindu commuters of bogey no. 6 of the railway train at Godhra in February 2002 which resulted not only in riots but also in temporary polarization of Hindus in Gujarat. As regards the riots in Mumbai in 1992-93, Muslims only started the riots because of the destruction of a structure called Babri Masjid, even though Muslims did not use it for religious purpose for long. Moreover I don't know wherefrom Mr Sen got the impression that the minorities were terrorized. I was there in Mumbai at that time and the fact is that the Hindus were terrorized and had there been no Shiv Sena I don't know what would have been the fate of Hindus in Mumbai as police showed their incapability in protecting them.

Next, even though I am not a member of RSS or BJP, nor have I taken any brief on their behalf, I will deal with his arguments about the political support of BJP as I find there are some fallacies in his arguments.

4

Hindu Civilization

BEFORE dealing with political support of BJP and the fallacies of Mr Sen's arguments, let us consider his comments on Hindutva. He says that although Hinduism is an ancient religion, Hindutva is quite a recent political movement and that the movement sees Hindutva (literally, "the quality of Hinduism") as a quintessential guide to "Indianness." Mr Sen has correctly defined the term Hindutva. The question is why should such a movement start only recently? It would have been much better had Mr Sen dealt with this aspect. The reason lays in the way the leaders who were at the helm of affairs at the time of India's Independence behaved. As stated earlier, instead of adopting the Western secularism, like that of UK or US, they adopted what I call minorityism in the name of secularism, calling it as Indian Secularism as if the definition of secularism changes with the state adopting it. The result is that the religious minorities were given special rights and privileges that are not available to the religious majority. This resulted not only in interreligious confrontation, but also in threatening disintegration of Hinduism. Ramakrishna Mission and Jains applied to the courts for declaring them as religious minorities different from Hinduism in order to get all the benefits that religious minorities are enjoying under our Constitution. The question is, if our state is a secular state, why should a religious community, irrespective of whether it is a majority or minority, be given special rights and privileges that are not enjoyed by other religious community/ies? Luckily the Hon. Supreme Court did not agree to their contention, and they continue to remain as Hindus. In no other state in the world the religious minority communities enjoy such rights and privileges as are bestowed on them under the Indian Constitution. And still these pseudo-seculars of ours are speaking of national integration while in practice they act for national disintegration. How can there be national integration when you differentiate between citizens in the name of Indian secularism and a certain group is bestowed with special rights and privileges that are not given to others? How can there be, in a secular democratic state, discrimination between citizens in the name of protecting the minorities? And in spite of adopting and having such discriminations between the citizens, those who are speaking of national integration are either living in a fool's paradise or are fooling others. After giving special rights and privileges for minorities and making reservations for certain castes and sub-castes, who will be ready to give up their special rights and privileges? And how can the other citizens who are not given such rights and privileges keep quiet and for how long? What is being preached and practised in India in the name of secularism surely does not encourage or lead to national integration. And that is exactly what is happening in India. Religious minorities along with those who are getting reservations have become privileged classes and instead of reducing the gap between them and others who are not privileged, the state and these politicians are bent on widening the same for short-term gains and power with the result that India is being divided not only on the basis of religions but also on the basis of castes and sub-castes, genders, places, languages, etc. This is the real cause for Hindutva movement but instead of finding out the real cause and suggesting the remedial steps Mr Sen only blames the resultant. Hindutva movement has started to preserve Hinduism from further disintegration as also to preserve the unity of India.

Now let us consider Mr Sen's comments on political support of BJP. From his comments it is apparent that for whatever reasons, he is fully prejudiced and biased against BJP and once a person is prejudiced, he loses his logic and common sense. I do not dispute the statistical data provided by Mr Sen on the number of seats owned by BJP and its allies in the past elections, but one thing should be noted that in the last election the Congress also could neither get an absolute majority nor even the number of seats owned by BJP in the earlier election when they formed the government. As regards "two-nation theory," Mr Sen blames Veer Savarkar for floating the idea first, but it is immaterial who floated the idea first, whether Muhammad Ali Jinnah or Veer Savarkar, the fact remains that it was ultimately accepted by Congress and India was divided on that basis. The question is why should Veer Savarkar float such an idea? Was it because of religions? Then he would have floated multi-nation idea since there were and are more than two religions in India. The reason for his floating the two-nation idea was that most of the Muslims behaved as if theirs is a separate nation, different from other Indians. They never freely mingled with others. Maybe because after 700 years of Muslim rule, they were thinking that they were the ruling class. This may be the reason for Veer Savarkar advancing the two-nation theory. Whatever may be the reason, in spite of the partition of India on the basis of religion and culture, still we find that Muslims as a class do not freely mingle or mix with other Indians. But one thing should never be forgotten and that is, Veer Savarkar was a great patriot.

Mr Sen's further remarks that "Nathuram Godse, who murdered Mahatma Gandhi for his failure to support the demands of Hindu politics of the day, was a disciple of Savarkar" are not in good taste to say the least. What is it that Mr Sen wants to imply by saying that Godse was a disciple of Savarkar? That it was Savarkar's plot to kill Mahatma Gandhi? It should be noted that the Court discharged Veer Savarkar after examining all the evidence. Had Savarkar been the author of the plot to kill the Mahatma he would have admitted it just like Godse who immediately surrendered after shooting the Mahatma without firing any shot at the public. So also I don't know from where Mr Sen got the information that Nathuram Godse murdered Mahatma Gandhi for his failure to support the demands of Hindu politics of the day. It is well known that Mahatma was killed by Godse because of his pressurizing the Indian government, by undertaking fast unto death, to pay to Pakistan Rs. 55 crore, which the Government of India had agreed to pay under an agreement but was refusing to pay till Pakistan vacates the aggression in Kashmir, and it was not for his failure to support the demands of Hindu politics of the day as alleged by Mr Sen.

Mr Sen's statistical argument is really perplexing. He says that BJP got support from a limited minority of the Hindus and that it has managed to get only about 22 per cent of total votes cast, in a country where more than 80 per cent of the total population happen to belong to the Hindu community. I don't understand why Mr Sen is stressing that BJP got only 22 per cent of the total votes cast. How many per cent the other major party got? It is only 27 per cent. And only because it has got less percentage of votes, is it precluded from taking the cause of a community if it feels that injustice is being done to such a community? And in a secular democracy, why should the number of votes cast by a particular religious community in favour of a particular party be important and be looked into? After all BJP is also a major political party like Congress. However as Mr Sen has raised the statistical argument, let us look into it. He says that in India more than 80 per cent are Hindus. I don't want to contradict his statement even though the fact is that the percentage of Hindus has come down to about 75 per cent. But even assuming that it is 80 per cent, the average vote cast in India is about 50 per cent. It is well known that the minority communities generally cast their votes on the advices of their religious authorities and on such advice almost everyone who is entitled to vote casts the vote. As such it can safely be presumed that the total votes cast by the minority communities in such elections is near about 100 per cent. That means 50 per cent of voters who are not casting their votes for whatever reasons are mostly Hindus. If we take away 50 per cent from the total 80 per cent of Hindu votes, what remains is 30 per cent. In other words if only 30 per cent of Hindus are casting their votes and if BJP gets even 22 per cent, it shows that majority of Hindus who have cast their votes have voted for BJP. And it cannot be taken for granted that those Hindus who have not voted at all are against BJP. Even though Mr Sen pretends that his irk is not against Hindus or Hinduism but against BJP and Sangh Parivar and those Hindu political activists who are bent on doing away with the broad and tolerant parts of Hindu tradition, the cat has come out of the bag and clearly shown his bias and prejudice against Hindus and Hinduism from his comments on the famous book *The Clash of Civilization and the Remaking of World Order* by Samuel Huntington where the author places India firmly in the category of "Hindu Civilization." Mr Sen, while putting him in the category of "intellectual simplifiers," says that in taking this peculiarly reductionist view, Huntington's perspective has to downplay the fact that India has many more Muslims than any other country in the world except Indonesia and marginally Pakistan and that nearly every country in Huntington's definition of "the Islamic civilization" has fewer Muslims than India has. I don't know whether Mr Sen is aware of the fallacy of his arguments. What does he want to signify by saying that every country in Huntington's definition of "the Islamic civilization" has fewer Muslims than India has? Does he want to indicate that as India has more Muslims than every other Muslim country coming under the definition of "the Islamic civilization," India should also come under the definition of "the Islamic civilization"? Does civilization depend upon the number of persons of religions or the ratio of persons of different religions a country has? Moreover he himself has said that more than 80 per cent of the total population of India happen to belong to the Hindu community which means that the Muslim population of India, even though maybe more than the Muslim population of any other Muslim country, is much less than 20 per cent of the total population of India. Further even these 20 per cent minorities have not come from outside but their forefathers were Hindus having the same civilization and as such even though they may follow Islam, their civilization cannot be other than Hindu civilization. It appears that in the case of "Hindu civilization," he wants to equate religions with cultures and civilizations even though he himself in his book *Identity and Violence* has admitted that there can be vast differences in the social behaviour of different persons belonging to the same religion even in the fields closely linked with religion because of cultural variations thus indirectly admitting the fact that civilization and culture of the persons even though belonging to the same religion can be different. Even then, it appears that Mr Sen has got objection to Huntington placing India in the category of "the Hindu civilization."

Further while describing Mr Huntington as "intellectual simplifier" and accusing him of downplaying the fact that India has many more Muslims than any other country in taking this peculiarly reductionist view, Mr Sen has not taken into consideration or has rather overlooked or ignored Mr Huntington's views and contentions that the central elements of any culture or civilization are language and religion and that unlike other civilizations (especially the Muslim civilization), but like Western civilization, only in Hindu civilization were religion and politics so distinctly separated (page 70) and that "if at some point India supplants East Asia as the world's economically most rapid developing area, the world should be prepared for extended disquisitions on superiority of Hindu culture, the contributions of the caste system to economic development, and how by returning to its root and overcoming the deadening Western legacy left by British imperialism, India finally achieved its proper place in the top rank of civilizations." Mr Sen also appears to have forgotten that Hindu civilization is not of recent origin. It was there much before not only the advent of Christianity and Islam in India but also their birth notwithstanding the now defunct theory of Aryan invasion of India. The only things which we, the Indians, irrespective of our religion, caste or race, should be proud of, is our legacy to our ancient Hindu culture, Hindu civilization and Hindu heritage. Moreover as stated earlier, it should be noted that even though Islam and Christianity are not of Indian origin and have come from outside, their followers in India were and are mostly of Indian origin having the same old Hindu civilization, culture and heritage. As regards the influence of Islamic civilization on Hindu civilization of India, even though our pseudo-seculars may claim that it is very much influenced by religious minority communities' civilization by attributing to them the qualities that they do not possess and as such places the Hindu civilization in the category of a composite civilization, I have clearly shown in my book *Can a Secular be a Fundamentalist?* that the influence of these civilizations on our Hindu civilization is almost negligible and even assuming that these civilizations possess the qualities attributed to them, then also since the Hindu civilization already possessed those qualities even before these civilizations came into existence, it cannot be said that our civilization was influenced by these civilizations for having those qualities. On the other hand, it can be said that the civilization of Indian Muslims even before Partition was a composite civilization since their civilization before the imposition of Islamic civilization on them was Hindu civilization and as such their new civilization is very much influenced by their earlier Hindu civilization. In any case, if we go through his book *The Clash of Civilizations*, we will find that he has seriously studied and considered the world civilizations including the Hindu civilization, and he cannot be classified as "intellectual simplifier" as described by Mr Sen. On the other hand, compared to Mr Huntington, Mr Sen himself appears to be an "intellectual simplifier," and his remarks about Mr Huntington appear to be casual and sweeping and without any proper basis.

Mr Sen is aware that something has gone wrong with his number-based assessment and therefore argues that the first difficulty in using the statistical argument is that a secular democracy that gives equal room to every citizen irrespective of religious background cannot be fairly defined in terms of the majority religion of the country and the second difficulty is that what is seen as a majority depends critically on what principle of classification is used. He further says that the people of India can be classified on the basis of different criteria, of which religion is only one and as an example he says that it is possible to classify Indians according to class, language, political beliefs, etc. Let us examine Mr Sen's statements carefully. He says that something goes wrong with the number-based assessment. But at the first place who has asked him to make number-based assessment? And it is only when he finds that the number-based assessment does not support his contentions, he says that something goes wrong. The difficulty appears to be that he is not clear in his mind as to what the word Hindu connotes. It should be noted that Hindus have not chosen to be called Hindus. Others have conceived the term and its definition and Hindus have simply found themselves carrying the label and gradually accepted it. It were the Persians who first used the term Hindu for the river Sindhu and the countries and inhabitants situated around and beyond it as the letter "S" in Sanskrit changes to "H" in ancient Persian. And as at that time all the inhabitants of the place were followers of Sanatana Dharma, the followers of Sanatana Dharma naturally came to be known as Hindus. Moreover as the Sanatana Dharma did not restrict its followers to worship a particular deity for getting self-realization or salvation or otherwise, there was no difficulty in following or worshipping the deity in any form the worshipper chooses. In fact, a follower of Sanatana Dharma generally worships three deities; one, the deity of the place, second, the deity of the family and the third, his chosen deity. And hence the term Hindu civilization, Hindu culture or Hindu heritage became the civilization, culture or heritage of the followers of Sanatana

Dharma, the inhabitants of the places and countries around the river Sindhu and beyond it, irrespective of the deity or the god chosen by such inhabitants. The difficulty arose when the Muslims and the Christians, the followers of Islam and Christianity respectively (which are in fact the *panths* or paths for salvation), started calling them as religions and each one insisted that its god is the only real god and its Prophet the only Prophet and did not agree with the Sanatana Dharma, that there can be different ways for getting self-realization or salvation or the god can be worshipped or prayed to in any form, the worshipper chooses. As such when Huntington places India firmly in the category of "the Hindu civilization" it is this ancient Hindu civilization of inhabitants of India and Sanatana Dharma and is not concerned with the present-day religions or the number of their followers. And that is why I insist that all Indians irrespective of religion, race or caste should be proud of being associated with such civilization.

It appears that Mr Sen's objection is to the word "Hindu" which Huntington used before the word "civilization" because of his bias and prejudice against Hindus and whatever is connected with Hindus and that is why he tried to justify his objection by number-based assessment, and when he could not succeed he says that something goes wrong and points out the difficulties as set out above. As regards his first difficulty I have already dealt with the same earlier and I do not want to repeat the same. As regards his second difficulty I feel it is beside the point and as such irrelevant except to prove one point — the title of his book *The Argumentative Indian* — he is after all an Indian. Next let us consider his comments on inventing the past and the rewriting of India's history.

5

Rewriting of Indian History — But by Whom?

LET us now see Mr Amartya Sen's views on inventing the past and rewriting the history, of course, by the Hindutva creed. He says that history is an active field of intellectual engagement for the Hindutva movement and parts of that movement have been very involved in the rewriting of history. He further says that it is worth enquiring why these issues are taken to be so central, as a result of which Indian history has become such a battlefield. He asks why is Hindutva politics so keen in redescribing the past? He himself answers it saying that the answer lies in two specific features of contemporary Hindu politics, viz. the first is the need to keep together its diverse components and to generate fresh loyalty from potential recruits. He says that the rewriting of India's history in line with the message of Hindutva is extremely important for the cohesion of the different elements of Sangh Parivar. The solidarity of the diverse members of the Sangh Parivar is greatly helped by taking a united view of India's history as essentially a "Hindu civilization." The second reason, he says, for focusing on India's past is the large support that comes from India's diaspora abroad for whom it is quite important to be able to retain their general Indian nationalist attachment.

He contends that following the electoral victory of coalition led by the BJP in 1998 and 1999, various arms of the government of India were mobilized in the task of arranging "appropriate" rewritings of Indian history. He further continues saying that even though this adventure of inventing the past is no longer "official" as BJP-led coalition was defeated in 2004, it is worth recollecting both because of what it tells us about the abuse of temporal power and also because of the light it throws on the intellectual underpinning of the Hindutva movement. He states that shortly after the BJP assumed office, the rapidly reorganized National Council of Educational Research and Training (NCERT) became busy not only in producing fresh textbooks for Indian school children, but also in deleting sections from books produced earlier under pre-BJP management by NCERT itself, written by reputed Indian historians.

Before commenting on his contentions, it appears that Mr Sen, like all other Hindu baiters, is allergic and intolerant to the word Hindu and whatever is connected with that word especially when somebody speaks of "Hindu civilization." It is rather surprising that a person, who was born and brought up as a Hindu, should become intolerant and allergic to the word Hindu. Perhaps while giving up the Hindu religion, Mr Sen also gave up tolerance, which, as he himself says is one of its characteristics. As regards Hindu civilization, as stated earlier, it is the oldest civilization, which was there even before the birth of Muslim or Christian civilizations. Of course, nowadays it is influenced by Western civilization.

No doubt, it is a fact that BJP-led coalition has not only reorganized NCERT and Indian Council of Historical Research (ICHR), but also produced fresh textbooks for Indian school children and deleted sections from books written by so-called reputed Indian historians. But the question is: were they the first to change and rewrite the history of India and why should they change the textbooks and delete section from books in such a hurry? Was there any reason for making such changes other than the ones set out by Mr Sen hereinabove? The answer lies in the fact that the earlier governments especially the Congress government had played and is still playing politics even in education and history. They did not correct the history when the modern historians challenged the theory of Aryan invasion of India on the basis of new discoveries both archaeological and ecological and proved that there was never any invasion of India by Aryans or Hindus as alleged by Max Müller and others and that the Hindus were the original inhabitants of India. Instead of looking into the matter and making fresh study by independent historians, these governments relied on the opinions of Marxist historians who had during all those periods infiltrated NCERT and ICHR and who for obvious reasons, did not agree with the modern historians and the new evidence produced by them. In any case, the basic question is whether the reconstituted NCERT was the first to rewrite the history or inventing the past as alleged by Mr Sen? Instead of giving some lame reasons to justify his allegations that Hindutva politics is keen in redescribing the past, had he juxtaposed the history he has learned in his school days against the history that was being taught after Independence of India, i.e. after these so-called reputed historians got appointments in ICHR and wrote the books on history, perhaps he would have found out that the Hindutva creed were not the pioneers in rewriting the history of India but the credit of rewriting the history and redescribing or inventing the past goes to Max Müller and these reputed historians unless he feels that whatever history he has learnt in his schools was only hearsay and not the actual history even though it was based on the actual records kept by Muslim historians and not any Hindu historian, and that the recorded history started only from the time these reputed historians (Marxist) wrote the Indian history. Of course, the honour of re-writing the history for the first time goes to the inventors of the theory of Aryan invasion of India.

If we read the Indian history written by the earlier Indian historians based on the records kept by earlier Muslim historians and others, before the infiltration of ICHR by these reputed historians, and their writing or rather rewriting the history of India, we will find out how these so-called reputed historians have distorted the history by changing, suppressing, misinterpreting and inventing and manipulating the historical facts. What BJP government tried to do was only to correct the distortions made by these historians and the inventors of the Aryan invasion theory. Of course, it was their mistake that they tried to correct the distortions in a hurry and thereby committed other mistakes. The proper course for BJP should have been to appoint a commission to find out the distortions made to the history as also the reasons for doing so. Then perhaps the cat would have come out of the bag and it would have known that what Mr Sen has spoken about the two specific features of contemporary Hindu politics really applies to these so-called reputed historians, who are really committed historians — committed to their communist ideology. Even though they are known as historians — professional historians, if those who are really interested in history read the books written by them, they will find out that these historians are not faithful to the real history but have distorted the history to suit their ideology. Of course, these historians who have infiltrated ICHR, because of their long association have now formed a sort of lobby, whose main aim is to defend their members if someone dares to criticize or contradict their work.

Their technique is simple. They have made each other famous by applauding each other's books. If any one is interested to know the atrocities and rape committed by them on the Indian history, one may read the book *Eminent Historians* by Arun Shourie. I have also written a booklet *Somanatha by Romila Thapar — A Critical Study* wherein I have tried to show how Romila Thapar in her book *Somanatha* published in 2002, has tried to whitewash the misdeeds of Mahmud Ghazni and to show him in a better light. It is not that these so-called reputed historians distorted, re-wrote and invented only the Indian history, but they also did the same thing with Hinduism or Sanatana Dharma. If one reads the book *Eminent Historians* of Arun Shourie, one can find out how these historians have played havoc with Hinduism by suppressing and distorting the facts about Hinduism. Firstly they do not call it as Hinduism or Sanatana Dharma but Brahmanism. Mr Shourie has quoted R.S. Sharma and Satish Chandra from their books *Ancient India* and *Medieval India* respectively to show how these so-called reputed historians have shamelessly distorted and suppressed the facts about Hinduism to bring it in line with and to confirm and prove their now-defunct theory of Marxism. They even forget that anyone who cares to read original books on Hinduism or historical records will find out the truth and their most pitiable attempt to hide the truth in order to prove their outdated ideology. Instead of finding out and doing research on why their pet theory has failed especially in India, these *manasputras* of Marx and slaves of Marxism try to prove their theory by hiding and suppressing and distorting the actual facts. In fact, before BJP-led government came to power and again after 2004 when Congress-led government came to power, when these reputed historians infiltrated ICHR, it has not remained the Indian Council of Historical Research as the name indicates, but Indian Council of Historical Distortion.

Mr Sen says that many Indians felt alarmed that Hindutva movement would stop at nothing short of alienating India from its own past through their control over schools and textbooks. I don't know, which Indians he is referring to. Perhaps they might have been those who have studied distorted history from the books written by these historians after Independence of India. Had they read and known the real history of India, they would not have been so alarmed. On the other hand, they would have been alarmed because of the distortions made by these historians to the Indian history. Even after the coming of the Congress-led government at the Centre in 2004 and reappointments of these historians in ICHR, NCERT has published the new revised history book demolishing old beliefs and trampling over heroes of history. It says "Prithviraj Chauhan was a coward who ran away to save his life during the second battle of Tarain with Mohammad Ghauri" and "Jaichand was in fact a 'hero' who gave up his life while fighting the forces of Ghauri." The book further says that when Prithviraj accepted the supremacy of Mohammad Ghauri, the latter allowed him to continue as ruler of Ajmer but was later killed on charges of treason and that Jaichand's valour was unmatched. The history, which was taught to us till now, says that Jaichand was a coward and traitor who betrayed Prithviraj Chauhan. And Mr Sen says that it is the Hindutva creed that is rewriting and inventing Indian history!

Mr Sen says that there are many outstanding historians in India and they have clearly a protective role to play. He suggests that it would be best if the defence of history comes from a genuine commitment to history, not just from political opposition to the Hindutva view. He further continues that there are many well-established and respected Indian historians who did question, with reasonable justification, the accuracy and authenticity of the claims made by Hindutva ideologues. The suggestion is very good and should be accepted. But the only question is who are the well-established and respected Indian historians he is referring to and whether the well-established and respected historians who did question the accuracy and authenticity of the claims made by Hindutva ideologues, are they genuinely committed to history or to their own ideologies? Because all the reputed historians he has referred to so far are committed to their own ideologies rather than to the history, and in their view, all other Indian historians are not reputed or professional but are pulp historians.

Next we will consider his views and comments on the nature of the problem that the BJP faced in trying to change India's past and the example given by him to illustrate the same.

6

Sen's Allegations against Hindutva

Now let us consider the nature of the problem, according to Mr Amartya Sen, that the BJP faced, in trying to change India's past. Let us examine his accusations and allegations against Hindutva in detail so as to see how they boomerang on him and his Marxist historian friends. He says that:

1. The "Indus Valley civilization," dating from the third millennium BCE, flourished well before the earliest Hindu literature, viz. the Vedas, which are typically dated in the middle of the second millennium BCE and that the Indus Valley civilization or the Harappa civilization had many special achievements, including remarkable town planning, organized storage especially for grains and extraordinary drainage system which, in his judgement, is unequalled in the following four thousand years in the subcontinent.
2. Even though there is obvious material here for national or civilizational pride of Indians, it poses an immediate problem for the Hindutva view of India's history, since an ancient civilization that is clearly pre-Sanskritic and pre-Hindu deeply weakens the possibility of seeing Indian history in pre-eminently and constitutively Hindu terms.
3. There is a further challenge, which relates to the arrival, most likely in the second millennium BCE, of the Indo-

Europeans, known as Aryans, riding horses (unknown in the Indus Valley Civilization) due to which the Hindutva view of history, which traces the origin of Indian civilization to the Vedas, has double difficulties, viz. (a) to accept that the fundamental basis of Hindu culture came originally from outside India and (b) not being able to place Hinduism at the beginning of Indian cultural history and its urban heritage.

4. Even though the Hindutva enthusiasts have been great champions of Vedic mathematics and Vedic sciences, which they allege to have been developed in ancient India, there is no sophisticated mathematics in the Vedas or anything that can be called rigorous science. And in spite of this, the BJP-created proposed history textbooks tried, with little reason and even less evidence, to place the origin of some of these contributions in the Vedic period.
5. In the Hindutva theory, much hangs on the genesis of the Vedas, in particular who composed them, were they composed later than Indus Valley civilization? He further ridicules the Hindutva theory saying that it would have been best for the Hindutva theory if the composers of Vedas were native Indians, settled in India for thousands of years, rather than Indo-Europeans coming from abroad and had the Vedas been composed earlier than the Indus Valley civilization in sharp contrast with the accepted knowledge. He also asks how ancient were the Vedic sciences and mathematics?
6. In view of the above, the Hindutva champions made attempts to rewrite Indian history in such a way that these disparate difficulties are simultaneously removed

by making the Sanskrit-speaking composers of Vedas also the same people who created the Indus Valley civilization which was accordingly renamed as "the Indus-Sarasvati civilization" in honour of the non-observable river called Sarasvati which is referred to in the Vedas. So also the intellectual origins of the Hindu philosophy as well as of the concocted Vedic science and Vedic mathematics are put solidly in the third millennium BCE, if not earlier.

7. The problem with this account is its obvious falsity going against all the available evidence based on archaeology and literature. In order to clarify the matter, he says that it is necessary to distinguish between three distinct errors that are conflated together in the invented history, viz.

    (a) the spurious claim of the indigenous origin of Sanskrit and the Vedas, denying their Indo-European roots,

    (b) the absurd belief in the Sanskrit-based nature of the Indus civilization despite all evidence to the contrary, and

    (c) the manifest affirmation that the Vedas contain much sophisticated mathematics and many scientific discoveries even though a non-partisan reader cannot find them there.

From the above, it is clear that all his allegations and contentions against Hindutva theory are solely based on his firm belief that there was Aryan invasion of India sometime in the second millennium BCE and that the Vedas were composed sometime in the middle of the second millennium BCE, which dates were arbitrarily determined by mainly Max Müller and others, without any basis whatsoever for obvious reasons which we shall discuss very soon. But before touching that part and discussing their intellectual crimes, let us consider the confession made by a source linked to the perpetrators of this crime, the startling disclosure made by the BBC website sometime back which must have given a shock to these supporters of Aryan invasion theory, like Mr Sen and his Marxist historian friends even though it might have been recanted by BBC subsequently for obvious reasons.

BBC said that there is now ample evidence to show that Max Müller and those who followed him were wrong. It says that even though the Aryan invasion theory was based on archaeological, linguistic and ethnological evidence, later research has either discredited this evidence or provided new evidence that combined with the earlier evidence makes other explanations likely. It also admits that modern historians of the area no longer believe that such invasions had such great influence on Indian history and that it is generally accepted that the Indian history shows a continuity of progress from the earliest times to today and that the changes brought to India by other cultures are no longer thought to be a major ingredient to the development of Hinduism. It also points out the dangers of the Aryan invasion theory, which denies the Indian origin of India's predominant culture, gives credit for the Indian culture to the invaders from elsewhere, teaches that the most revered Hindu scriptures are not actually Indian and devalues India's culture by portraying it as less ancient than it actually is. *BBC further says that the theory of Aryan invasion was not just wrong but included unacceptably racist ideas which suggested or asserted that*:

- Indian culture was not a culture in its own right but a synthesis of elements from other cultures;
- Hinduism was not authentically Indian in origin, but the result of cultural imperialism;

- Indian culture was static and only changed under outside influence;
- the Dravidians were a nobody and got their faith from the Aryan invaders;
- the indigenous people could acquire new ideas only from invaders or other races;
- race was a biological, not a social concept;
- the north Indian people descended from invaders from Europe and as such socially were closer to the British; and
- the British were reforming India like the Aryans did thousands of years earlier thus justifying the role and status of the Raj.

Finally it says that the theory downgraded the intellectual status of India and its people by giving falsely a later date to the elements of Indian science and culture.

It is pertinent to note that all this is said not by Hindutva champions or Sangh Parivar but by BBC, a source linked to the ex-colonizers, the very perpetrators of wrong theory, which has played havoc in the Indian history. I presume that the above disclosure by BBC takes care of all the accusations and allegations of Mr Sen against Hindutva and BJP especially his allegations about rewriting of Indian history by Hindutva champions and now it is for him and his Marxist friends to defend.

Even though BBC has now made the startling disclosure that there was never the so-called Aryan invasion of India and acknowledged the mistake, it is doubtful whether these renowned but committed Marxist historians of Mr Sen's will agree to the same on the ground of their usual lame excuse that the findings of BBC are based on the writings of historians who did not observe historical methods and procedures of analysis and as such it is not acceptable to professional historians as if the discoveries and inventions made by these historians are vitiated only because they did not follow the method and procedure of analysis acceptable to these so-called professional historians. And what are these methods and procedure of analysis, these professional historians only know. The fact is that they are clinging to this theory — the theory of Aryan invasion of India — not because they are convinced that there was really an Aryan invasion of India, but because it gives them a chance to prove their ideology of Marxism, which is based on the theory of oppressor and oppressed and class struggle which was not only unsuccessful when applied to Indian conditions, but also rejected by countries which initially had accepted and have followed the same, viz. Russia and China. These *manasputra*s of Karl Marx and slaves of Marxism like faithful *pativrata*s still believe in the Marx ideology and feel that if they can prove that there was in fact the Aryan invasion of India even by rewriting the Indian history as is being done by them, and that these barbaric Aryans who invaded India (as per the original theory), not only pushed the original inhabitants, the Dravidians, to the south after destroying their culture and civilization, but also made them join as members of the lowest caste (as per the original theory), they will still be able to prove Marx's theory (of class struggle) which ideology has now become otherwise defunct and has been rejected by the world. I, therefore, in spite of the disclosures made by BBC as above, now propose to examine each point and issue raised by Mr Sen, each allegation made by him against the Hindutva and each of his statement set out hereinabove.

He says that the "Indus Valley civilization," dating from the third millennium BCE, flourished well before the timing of the earliest Hindu literature, the Vedas, which are typically dated in the middle of the second millennium BCE. And on such assumptions, as if they are the gospel truth and that everyone has accepted them, he alleges that the Hindu champions have attempted to rewrite the history making the Sanskrit-speaking composers of the Vedas the very same people who created the Indus Valley civilization. But even amongst different Gospels there is no uniformity. He neither gives any independent proof or evidence for his allegations and acceptance of the theory of Aryan invasion and for dating the Vedas in the middle of second millennium BCE, nor contradicts or challenges the contentions of present-day historians especially when the theory of Aryan invasion is seriously challenged, and the composition of the Vedas is taken two or three millennium earlier by them on the basis of fresh proof and evidence discovered. If it is shown that there was in fact no Aryan invasion of India and it was a myth created for obvious reasons, all his allegations and comments will fall to the ground. Not only that but it will boomerang on him and those renowned historians who still insist that there was such an invasion, on the basis of whose writings he has made the allegations. As such, before discussing and scrutinizing his accusations, allegations and comments it is necessary to examine afresh the theory of Aryan invasion and the assumed chronology of Vedic India in the light of fresh evidence produced as also the evidence on the basis of which it was assumed that there was Aryan invasion of India. Let us now consider what is this theory of Aryan invasion of India, who invented it, whether there was any purpose in inventing it, whether there were sufficient grounds or evidence to claim that Aryans were not the original inhabitants of India and all other related matters.

7

Aryan Invasion of India Reconsidered

Now let us consider what is known as the theory of Aryan invasion of India. The theory says that the Hindus — called in the theory as Aryans — were not the original inhabitants of India as the British are, and had invaded India many many years before. In short the Aryans were the carbon copy of European colonizers. The main inventor of the theory was one Max Müller, a German living in England. The theory has taken many turns and twists in due course. Initially the invading Aryans were considered to be blond and blue-eyed while the original inhabitants — the Dravidians — were said to be dark skinned. The invasion is said to have taken place around 1500 BCE and that the composition of Vedas began in or about 1200 BCE. However, no bases for such determinations were given. If one studies the theory in detail, one will wonder how such a half-baked theory, which was entirely based on speculations, was accepted at all. Whether there was any purpose in formulating the theory, we will consider later on. First let us consider the theory itself. As stated above, being speculative in nature, it has changed its face so many times with the result that what we see now is entirely different from the one when it was formulated, and it will be interesting to see how it changed its face from time to time.

It says the Aryans invaded India in the middle of second millennium BCE. How the word Aryan was used for Hindus is a mystery. Just like the name Hindu was given by outsiders and Hindus never called themselves as Hindus, similarly the inventors of the theory introduced the word Aryan for Hindus. Hindus never called themselves as Aryans in its vast literature. The word Aryan was used to denote noble birth and not to denote a race. Initially, as stated above, the theory was based upon the idea that the Aryans belonged to a particular racial stock and spoke Vedic Sanskrit, and they overthrew the primitive and aboriginal culture of the time — the Dravidian culture — and brought a more advanced civilization to India. This was prior to the discovery of Indus Valley civilization in 1920. In fact, the theory was invented to solve the problem of languages. Linguists found similarities between Sanskrit and European languages. As a consequence, the origin and spread of Indo-European languages was confounded with the race theory as stated above. Subsequently, it was claimed that Europeans and Aryans were different branches of a common stock known as Indo-Europeans with their homeland somewhere in Central Asia or even Europe. Even today, the supporters of the invasion theory cannot pinpoint the exact place of their original homeland nor have they produced any supporting evidence whatsoever for their claim. There is no archaeological evidence for their claim nor do they give any reason for claiming migration of the two branches of the so-called Indo-European stock to Europe and India respectively. It appears that all of a sudden, the people decided for no apparent reason, to leave their place of residence and migrate to other places without leaving any trace at the place of their original stay. Everything is speculative which they want us to believe.

Even this racial theory did not remain for long. Shortly after the Franco-Prussian war, Max Müller who was mainly responsible for the theory made a volte-face and said *"I have declared again and again that if I say Aryan, I mean neither blood nor bones, nor skull nor hair; I mean simply those who speak Aryan language."* (Max Müller 1888: p. 120). However the historical record does not permit this negation of its racial origins, as stated by Sir Julian Huxley (*Race in Europe,* 1939, Oxford Pamphlet No. 5, OUP, p. 9). "Moreover, Max Müller threw another apple of discord. He introduced a proposition, which is demonstrably false. He spoke not only of a definite Aryan language and its descendants, but also of a corresponding "Aryan race"."

However this original theory that Aryans invaded India and said to have overthrown the primitive and aboriginal culture, which was thought to be Dravidian in nature, and brought an advanced civilization, has again undergone a change when in 1920 what is now called "the Indus Valley civilization" was discovered. By now it was accepted as an established fact that the Aryan invasion had taken place in 1500 BCE and Vedas were composed thereafter, and since Indus Valley civilization (Harappa and Mohenjo-Daro) was discovered and excavated subsequently, it was uncritically accepted that the Indus Valley civilization must be pre-Vedic. And the early archaeologists like John Marshall and Mortimer Wheeler, on the basis of the Aryan invasion theory, misinterpreted the Indus site in terms of the theory that the Harappa and Mohenjo-Daro were destroyed and ruined because of the Aryan invasion and these interpretations were offered as proof of the theory. Because of this discovery, the Aryan invasion theory was rewritten to make the Aryans as the uncivilized nomadic and barbarian destroyers of the civilized Dravidian-Harappan culture. So now, the Dravidian culture which was earlier supposed to be primitive and aboriginal, became a civilized culture and the Aryans who were earlier considered to be more civilized, now became uncivilized barbarians. The theory however has undergone further modification when it was discovered that the sites at Harappa were abandoned rather than destroyed by Aryans, because of major ecological changes in the region, shifting of the rivers and drying up of the Sarasvati river. The supporters of the theory now began to say that there was no invasion by ferocious and barbaric Aryans and no destruction of the Indus Valley civilization as it was thought to be, but only migration by mild pastoral Aryans.

From the above it is very clear that the theory is not based on any hard archaeological evidence but purely on speculation, the only evidence, if at all it can be considered as evidence, is philological, that is the similarity of languages. In fact, the logical and natural reason for similarity of languages can be because of contacts between the two people — Europeans and Indians, or it may be because there might have been migration of some Indians from India to Europe, which possibilities were never considered, maybe intentionally. Moreover from the haste in accepting and popularizing the theory, one gets a strong feeling that the purpose of formulating the theory was quite different, which we shall consider later on. At present we will see the shortcomings of the theory.

Before considering the defects of the theory, one thing should be noted and that is, before the invention of the theory in the nineteenth century, no doubt was raised by anyone about the Hindus being the original inhabitants of India, nor was there any collective memory amongst the Hindus either about the invasion or migration to India from some place outside India. The vast Vedic literature also provides no evidence whatsoever about the foreign origin of its writers. Even the supporters of the theory had to admit that the theory has no basis in Sanskrit literature. T. Burrow admits that *the Aryan invasion of India is recorded in no written document and it cannot yet be traced archaeologically*. (*A Cultural History of India*,

Clarendon Press, 1975, p. 21). B.K. Ghosh, also an exponent of the theory admits that *it really cannot be proved that the Vedic Aryans retained any memory of their extra-Indian association* and also refers to the *total absence of extraterritorial memory in the Rigveda*. (*History and Culture of Indian People*, vol. I, *The Vedic Age*, ed. R.C. Majumdar). Is it not surprising that the eminent historian Romila Thapar, who was very keen to give a clean chit to Mahmud Ghazni because of the absence of reference to destruction of Somanatha temple by Mahmud in any of the Sanskrit inscriptions found at the place, did not consider similar evidence as a proof against the acceptance of the invasion theory? The fact is that before the invention of the invasion theory and rewriting of Indian history by Max Müller and others in the nineteenth century, everyone, including Hindus themselves, considered Hindus as original inhabitants of India. Now let us consider the defects of the theory.

1. As stated above, the theory is purely and entirely based on one premise, philological, that is similarity of some words in European languages and Sanskrit, which, at the most can be considered speculative evidence, and without support or verification by other sources cannot carry any weight at all. There is no other evidence whatsoever archaeological, literary, ecological or otherwise supporting the theory even though the supporters of the theory try to misinterpret the evidence.

2. The exponents of the theory imagined and modified the theory to claim that Europeans and Aryans were different branches of a common stock of people known as Indo-Europeans coming from Central Asia or Europe again purely on speculations without any evidence whatsoever. Till today they could not pin-point the definite home of such common stock or give

any evidence archaeological or otherwise of existence of such a place.

3. When Indus Valley civilization was discovered in 1920, they thought that they got the necessary evidence supporting their theory and modified the theory making the Aryans, who were earlier supposed to be more civilized, becoming barbarians and uncivilized who destroyed the then existing civilization of Dravidians, the original inhabitants of India. But their joy was short-lived when it was found that the Harappan civilization was in fact not destroyed, but the place was deserted because of the drying up of the river on whose banks the whole civilization existed, and they again modified the theory saying that there was no invasion by the ferocious Aryan hordes but only migration of pastoral Aryans coming with herds of cattle. This again is based on speculation.

4. In spite of the fact that the theory, as stated above, is based only on linguistic evidence which is at the best a speculative evidence, its proponents and supporters admit only such supporting evidence which does not cast any doubt on the theory. They reject as unacceptable without examination, the readings of the Indus script by S.R. Rao, one of the foremost authorities of the world on Indus archaeology, Subhash Kak and others only because they failed to support the theory. When late in the eighteenth century Lokmanya Tilak (1893) and Jakobi (1894) identified astronomical statements in the *Rigveda* and other ancient works that cast serious doubts on their chronology, they were rejected as unreliable. When archaeological finds have begun to suggest the presence of Vedic Aryans in India

centuries and even millennia before their presumed arrival in India, historians of this school continue to reject these suggestions, citing "linguistic evidence" as more conclusive and reliable. (*Vedic Aryans and the Origins of Civilization*, Navaratna S. Rajaram and David Frawley)

5. Apart from the fact that the theory is based on speculative evidence, the dates on which the so-called invasion is said to have taken place (1500 BCE) and the Vedas were composed (1200 BCE) were arbitrarily fixed without any basis. Perhaps, Max Müller who was responsible for fixing the dates, being a devout Christian, might have been strongly influenced by the Biblical belief that the world was created at 9:00 a.m. on 23 October 4004 BCE, and might have fixed the dates taking into consideration the above belief. But the fact remains that he has not given any basis or evidence for fixing such dates. Subsequently, however, under pressure from critics he even disowned his chronology.

K.C. Verma (*Mahabharata: Myth and Reality — Differing Views*, ed. S.P. Gupta and K.S. Ramachandran) quotes the following admissions by Max Müller:

"I need hardly say that I agree with almost every word of my critics. I have repeatedly dwelt on the entirely hypothetical character of the dates I ventured to assign to the first three periods of Vedic literature. All I have claimed for them has been that they are minimum dates.

"If now we ask how we can fix the date of these three periods, it is quite clear that we cannot fix *a terminus a quo*. Whether the Vedic hymns were composed 1000 or 2000 or 3000 years BCE, no power on earth will ever determine." As K.C. Verma points out: "All attempts to date the Vedic literature on linguistic grounds have failed miserably for the simple reason that *(a) the conclusions of comparative philology are often speculative and (b) no one has yet succeeded in showing how much change should take place in a language in a given period. The only safe method is astronomy.*" (From *Aryan Invasion Theory and Indian Nationalism*, Shrikant G. Talageri, pp. 171-72)

In spite of linguistics and logical constraints as above, the supporters of the theory, it appears, still feel that philological principles and rules are more scientific and should be applied to Vedas. As per the arguments of B.K. Ghosh: "From a purely linguistic point of view, the *Rigveda* in its present form cannot be dated much earlier than 1000 BCE. The language of the *Rigveda* is certainly no more different from that of the Avestan Gathas than is Old English from Old High German and therefore they must be assigned the same age." The question is, how can the philological principles and rules formulated on the basis of study of certain languages, especially European, can be applied to Sanskrit language, especially when there was oral transmission where importance and stress is given not only to the words but also to pronunciations and tones etc.? In such a case how can one determine the age of the language, where everything remains the same, whether the language is of recent origin or of thousands or millions of years earlier on the basis that another language which is of recent origin, is similar to that language? In spite of this, ever since fixing of the date of *Rigveda* by Max Müller at 1000 BCE, the protagonists of the invasion theory treat this date as sacrosanct almost as if this was the date written in the *Rigveda* itself.

Next we will see how the theory has been riddled with paradoxes.

8

Paradoxes of Aryan Invasion Theory Considered

SINCE the inception of the theory of Aryan invasion of India, it is riddled with paradoxes, which the inventors of the theory or its supporters are unable to explain satisfactorily. And when they try to explain the things, they create further problems than they solve.

1. The Harappans of the Indus Valley have left profuse archaeological records over a vast region, from the borders of Iran and beyond Afghanistan to Eastern Uttar Pradesh and the Tapti Valley, which, as per the supporters of the theory, are Dravidian records. And yet these people have left absolutely no literary records. On the other hand, the Vedic Aryans and their successors have left us a literature that is probably the largest in the world, but as per the theory, there is absolutely no historical or archaeological record that they ever existed anywhere in the world, not even at the place from where they are supposed to have migrated. It is a peculiar case of a literature without a history or archaeology and a history or archaeology without a literature. A further thing to be noted is that even though the supporters of the theory consider the Harappan civilization as Dravidian, the earliest Dravidian literature (Tamil) dates from not earlier than

the first century BCE. This has complicated the matter in the sense that we have been told that Harappans were literate while the invading barbaric Aryans were supposedly not, and in spite of this, the literature that has survived is that of illiterate(?) Aryans and not of cultured and literate(?) Harappans (Dravidians).

2. We have been told by Mr Amartya Sen and others that the Harappan civilization had many special achievements including remarkable town planning, organized storage and extraordinary drainage system (unequalled in the subcontinent in the following four thousand years as per Mr Sen) and the world had to wait for about two thousand years until the Roman Empire, before town planning and sanitation attained the same level as in Harappan cities. At the same time the proponents of the theory tell us that the Indians borrowed geometry and astronomy from the Greeks following Alexander's invasion of India. As per Mr Sen even with the Vedas, which were alleged to have been composed in or about 1000 BCE, there is no sophisticated mathematics in them, or anything that can be called rigorous science. There were much of them in India only in the first millennium CE. The question is, if that is the case, and Indians knew no geometry before Alexander, how could they construct such a remarkable city with carefully laid-out streets and drainage system before 2000 BCE, without knowing A, B, C, of geometry or arithmetic which they could study only in or about CE 1000?

3. There is another paradox about the language — the Sanskrit language. We have been told that the Aryans who had first invaded India were uncivilized, uncultured and illiterate nomadic barbarians. But when

the Western scholars studied the Sanskrit language they were rather puzzled as to how Aryans whose language was supposed to be Sanskrit could be uncivilized and barbarians. In late eighteenth century, Sir William Jones (1746-94) has noted *". . . the Sanskrit language, whatever be its antiquity, is of wonderful structure, more perfect than Greek, more copious than Latin, and more exquisitely refined than either."* (Jones 1806: p. 420). So also the American scholar Vyaas Houston, commenting in particular about the *Rigveda* and its language remarked: *"where did it come from? — a language infinitely more sophisticated than any of our modern tongues. How could language have been so much more refined in ancient times, especially among a people, the Vedic Aryans, who scholars tell us, were nomadic barbarians from the north? The discrepancy between the language and what has been offered as its origin is so great that either we are thoroughly at a loss, or have tended at times to resort to supernatural explanations. The obvious truth is there must have been an equally refined and advanced civilization."* (Frowley 1991: p. 11)

4. Another puzzle is about the river Sarasvati, which is described in *Rigveda* in glowing terms. Here the supporters of the invasion theory find themselves in a dilemma. If they admit that it is the description of the river Sarasvati before it dried up and when it was flowing in full vigour and force in or about third or fourth millennium BCE, they will have to admit that their chronology about the composition of the Vedas and Aryan invasion of India is not correct which will ultimately raise a question mark about the theory itself. So in order to protect and save the theory they allowed their imagination to run wild and amok

thereby giving a goodbye to logic and common sense. I will give in a nutshell how Romila Thapar has described it in her book *The Penguin History of Early India* (published by Penguin Books India, 2003).

She speaks about the river Hakra that is thought to have once been a significant river flowing almost parallel with the Sutlej and the lower Indus, with its estuary in the Rann of Kutch. However the waters of its upper reaches, sometimes called the Ghaggar, were diverted through natural hydraulic changes. So also rivers originally flowing into the Hakra were converted into the Sutlej, becoming a tributary of the Indus and linked to the Beas and the Yamuna, joining the Ganges. The gradual drying up of the Hakra of which all that remained are the disjointed streams of the present-day Ghaggar followed this. Her further statements are mischievous. She says that the identification of Ghaggar with the Sarasvati is controversial and indicates that the early references to Sarasvati in the *Rigveda* could be the Haraxvati Plain in Afghanistan and that the identification is also problematic as the Sarasvati is said to cut its way through high mountains, which is not the landscape of Ghaggar. She claims that although the Sarasvati is described in the *Rigveda* in glowing terms, the Sutlej and the Yamuna were already separate rivers and not flowing into the Ghaggar, which indicates that the hymns were composed subsequent to the changes affecting the Hakra/Ghaggar. She philosophizes and makes a general statement that once the river is mythologized through invoking the memory of the earlier river, its name — Sarasvati — could be applied to many rivers.

It is necessary to discuss and dissect her statements in detail to show her intellectual dishonesty and hypocrisy. Firstly she calls the river that has dried up, as Hakra and not the Sarasvati even though from the context of *Rigveda* it appears that what has been referred to in the *Rigveda* as Sarasvati, is the same river, which she refers to as Hakra even though what has remained in Ghaggar after drying of Hakra, she calls as Sarasvati. This is only because, if she admits that Hakra is the same, which is referred to in the *Rigveda* as Sarasvati, her whole chronology and the theory of Aryan invasion collapses and falls to the ground. Her statement that the early reference to Sarasvati in the *Rigveda* could be to Haraxvati Plain in Afghanistan is nothing but a figment of her imagination that has run amok. For, as per her theory, the first Vedas, the *Rigveda* was composed in or about 1200 BCE, that is about 300 years after the invasion of India by Aryans. As such the composers of Vedas were many generations after the invasion and must not have seen Afghanistan or the river Haraxvati. In such a situation, how can it be said that the description of the river Sarasvati in the *Rigveda* is through invoking the memory of the earlier river, which the composers have not seen? Secondly, is the river Haraxvati in Afghanistan so big and mighty or was it so earlier, as is described in *Rigveda* as the river Sarasvati? Thirdly reference to the river Sarasvati in the *Rigveda* is not isolated. It describes the topography of the Vedic land as the land of seven rivers. It also places the Sarasvati between the Yamuna and Sutudri (modern Sutlej, *RV*, X.75.5) or between Yamuna and Parusni (modern Ravi), where this great dried up river has been found. So also *Yajurveda, Vajasaneya Samhita,* speaks of five rivers feeding the Sarasvati and making it into a great river:

> Five rivers converge in the Sarasvati along with its streams. The Sarasvati becoming fivefold in that region became a vast river."
>
> — *Sukla Yajurveda* 34.19 (from *Vedic Aryans and the Origin of the Civilization* by N.S. Rajaram and David Frawley)

In the circumstances how can it be said that the references to Sarasvati in the *Rigveda* could be to the Haraxvati Plain in Afghanistan? Is the topography of the place described in the *Rigveda* similar to one found in Afghanistan? Further there is a typical verse in the *Rigveda* that says: "*Sarasvati, the best of mothers, the best of rivers, the best goddess. . . .*" (*RV*, 11.41.16 translation by N.S. Rajaram). The question is, why will the composers of *Rigveda* describe a river, which they have not seen, from a place they have never visited, in such terms calling it as best of mothers? They would have rather described the river on whose bank they have settled, viz. Ganges or Indus. And if the description of the river given in *Rigveda* were of Ganges or Indus on whose banks they have settled, then why would they call it as Sarasvati?

No doubt, as she says, the identification of the Ghaggar with the Sarasvati is controversial. But who has identified the Ghaggar with the Sarasvati? *Rigveda* has never identified the Ghaggar with the river Sarasvati. The description of Sarasvati in the *Rigveda* does not match even slightly with that of Ghaggar, which are disjointed streams that have remained after drying up of the river Hakra as described by Romila

Thapar herself. It is the supporters of the theory only, who are identifying Ghaggar with Sarasvati at the same time claiming that it is controversial. The whole question would not have arisen if the river Hakra before drying, when it was flowing with full vigour when it has cut its way through high mountains, was identified with the river Sarasvati as described in the *Rigveda*. But in that case, as stated above, the whole chronology of events as described by the supporters of the theory had to be changed. And in order not to change the chronology and to support the theory, they have tried to change the facts giving full scope to their imaginations. They have treated the invasion theory and the chronology of events that the invasion has taken place in or about 1500 BCE and the Vedas were composed from 1200 BCE, once formulated, as the established facts and interpreted the subsequent findings as deriving from it. So the contentions of Romila Thapar that the Sutlej and Yamuna were already separate rivers and not flowing into the Ghaggar when the *Rigveda* was composed, are on the basis that it was composed in or about 1200 BCE and not earlier. But the logic of her further argument is perplexing. She says that this indicates that the hymns were composed subsequent to the changes affecting the Hakra/Ghaggar. Earlier she herself, on the basis that the *Rigveda* composed in or about 1200 BCE was an established fact, said that it was composed after the Sutlej and Yamuna were separated and not flowing in the Ghaggar. And now she argues that this indicates that the hymns were composed subsequent to the changes affecting Hakra/Ghaggar. This only confirms what N.S. Rajaram and David Frawley have stated in their book *Vedic Aryans and the Origins of Civilization*. They have stated (on p. 11): "The basic point to be noted is that the theory (of the invasion) once formulated was treated as an established fact, and all subsequent findings were interpreted as deriving from it. And these interpretations were themselves later offered as proof of the theory. . . . This is called a tautology or a circular argument."

5. Another paradox is the interpretation given to the Sanskrit word *samudra* appearing in *Rigveda* by the supporters of the theory. The historians who support the said Aryan invasion theory have based the theory not only on linguistic evidence but also on literary interpretation of the Vedic literature. But as they are neither linguists nor Vedic scholars, they have based their contentions on the translations of the Vedic literature available to them, viz. that of Max Müller and of Griffith, which say that the *Rigveda* describes north-western India and Afghanistan, and that it does not know of any ocean, even though *Rigveda* itself contradicts this assumption. But this made them to interpret *samudra* as a pool of water and not as ocean. They further assumed that the authors of the *Rigveda* were nomadic barbarians from the steppes of central Asia, unfamiliar with the ocean and that the ocean is unknown to the *Rigveda* ignoring the fact that the word *samudra* has occurred very frequently in the *Rigveda* and in an overwhelming majority of cases *samudra* can only mean ocean or sea as seen from a passage of *Rigveda "The flow of our devotions hasten to him, like rivers to a vast ocean."* RV, 1.52.4 (from *Vedic Aryans and the Origin of Civilization*). In fact, intimate knowledge of ships, wind patterns and rain causing monsoon winds

was part of daily knowledge of the people of *Rigveda* that can be seen from different passages of *Rigveda*. The idea that the Aryans were unfamiliar with the sea is a fallacy created by these people without any basis especially from *Rigveda*, neither there is any writing in the *Rigveda* to support their contention that Aryans have come from Iran or Central Asia through the mountain passes of Afghanistan. Their whole theory of Aryan invasion of India is based purely on philology, which, at the best can be called a speculative science if it can be called a science at all, without any other proof or evidence from any other quarter. On the other hand, whatever discoveries are made subsequent to the invention of the theory, all go against the theory even though the supporters of the theory try to misinterpret, manipulate or alter the same, especially the literature using linguistic models whose validity is disputed by modern linguists themselves, and stoutly deny all data from archaeology, astronomy and any inferences that follow therefrom.

Next we will consider why such a half-baked theory, which is neither supported by any archaeological evidence nor any astronomical, topographical, literary or any other evidence from any quarters, and which is formulated purely on the basis of the so-called philological evidence which at the best can be considered only as a secondary evidence which, in normal course is required to be supported by primary evidence as it is of speculative in nature, became so popular and famous and was accepted as established fact immediately on its formulation.

9

The Reasons for Inventing the Theory

GENERALLY, whenever a popular belief is to be replaced by a new theory, it is required to be supported by strong evidence. Not only that but it is required to be proved beyond any doubt before it is accepted. But in case of the Aryan invasion theory, in spite of there being no positive and concrete evidence in its favour except the so-called philological evidence which, as stated earlier, at the best is a speculative evidence, and on the other hand whatever evidence literary, astronomical, archaeological, topographical and all other that are found and discovered go against the theory, the theory was immediately accepted as established fact. Not only that but even now, whenever new evidence is discovered that goes against the theory, the supporters of the theory immediately dismiss it as unreliable without going through the evidence or discussing it, on the lame excuses that historical methods were not observed or procedures were not followed, etc. This raises a doubt whether the theory is the outcome of a serious and honest research on the part of its proponents or it is a carefully manipulated plan to discredit Hindus and Hinduism for obvious reasons and with certain purposes. In order to find out the truth, it is necessary to study the circumstances under which the theory was formulated, whether there was any other purpose in formulating the theory than pure research to find out the truth, whether the person who invented the theory was influenced by any other consideration than historical research, etc. Let us consider the above points one by one.

1. The theory of Aryan invasion of India was invented when the British who had taken over virtually the whole of India, were in need of justifying their occupation of India especially after the 1857 events, and the theory provided them the necessary justification by claiming that the Aryans (Hindus) who were considered to be the original inhabitants of India, were also not the original inhabitants and like British, they had also invaded India and had occupied the same maybe thousands of years earlier. Not only that, the Dravidians who were supposed to be the earlier occupants of India, were also not the original occupants but like Aryans they had also came to India much earlier than Aryans. Similarly now the British claim to have occupied India like the Dravidians and Aryans.
2. The missionaries with their proselytizing zeal have found it very much in their interest to join hands with the government which led to European missionaries studying Sanskrit, and the proselytizing activities of European missionaries which the British authorities actively encouraged, had a colonial motive as seen by men like Thomas Babbington Macaulay whose influence is still felt in higher education in India and who believed that the spread of Christianity would help in the efficient administration of India. He was instrumental in establishing a network of modern English schools in India one of whose goals was the conversion of Hindus to Christianity. He believed that knowledge and reflection on the part of the Hindus

would cause them to give up their age-old belief in favour of Christianity and to this end he wanted someone who would interpret Indian scriptures in such a way that newly educated Indians would see for themselves the difference between their scriptures and the New Testament and choose the latter, and he was fortunate to find such a person in Max Müller.

3. Max Müller was a devout Christian who believed that the end of spreading his faith justified any means and though he was never a missionary in the literal sense, his work was infused with the missionary spirit. Further his motives are particularly hard to fathom since he seems to have been careful to conceal his true intentions from the way he shifted his positions to suit circumstances. Macaulay told him that the then East India Company, the predecessor of British Government of India, would be prepared to fund him if he could undertake to translate the *Rigveda* in such a manner that it would destroy the belief of Hindus in the Vedic religion and Max Müller agreed for the sake of Christianity to work for the company (*Vedic Aryans and the Origin of Civilization*, N.S. Rajaram and David Frawley). It was this Max Müller, who, though a scholar, was an agent of British government paid to advance its colonial interests, who was more than anyone else responsible for the invention of the theory of Aryan invasion of India and for the absurdly late Vedic chronology — dating of the *Rigveda* to 1200 BCE even though under pressure from critics, he later on admitted that whether the Vedic hymns were composed in 1000, 1500 or 2000 or 3000 BCE, no power on earth will ever determine. He is the same Max

> Müller who while writing about his translation of the *Rigveda* to his wife in 1866 had observed: " . . . *This edition of mine and the translation of Veda, will hereafter tell to a great extent on the fate of India and the growth of millions of souls of that country. It is the root of their religion and to show them what the root is, I feel sure, is the only way of uprooting all that has sprung from it during the last three thousand years.*" (Max Müller 1902, 1: 346). This and the contents of his letter written in 1868 to the Duke of Argyle that "*The ancient religion of India is doomed, and if Christianity does not step in, whose fault will it be?*" (Max Müller 1902, I: p. 378) clearly show his motives and his desire to uproot Indian tradition.

From the above it will be very clear that only because of the British government's interest which was entirely practical and political that such a half-baked theory which is based only on philological evidence which, as stated earlier, is of speculative nature, and in spite of contrary evidence that was found or discovered (archaeological, literary, ecological or otherwise), became not only popular but was immediately accepted as established fact. Of course, the so-called reputed Marxist historians support the theory because they feel that the theory of Aryan invasion of India supports their ideology of class struggle.

The theory and the arbitrary fixing of the Vedic chronology played havoc not only in Hindu culture and civilization but also in Hinduism itself. Many of the achievements of the Hindu civilization are attributed not to Hindus but to their non-existent predecessors, before their arrival in India. The Indian civilization, which is in fact the Hindu civilization, became a composite civilization and people like Mr Sen speaks of the role that Hindu tradition may have played in sustaining a dialogic culture and the tolerance of heterodoxy in India without explaining which Hindu tradition and culture he is speaking about, whether such a separate Hindu tradition and culture was in existence at all, at any time which is separate from and other than the dialogic civilization and culture he is speaking about. In fact, such a question of finding out the role played by Hindu tradition should not have been there when there was no such separate Hindu tradition or culture described anywhere. Further by arbitrary fixing of Vedic chronology as shown earlier, many questions and paradoxes have been created in the Vedic literature as pointed out earlier, which the supporters of the theory and the chronology cannot solve, and when they try to solve the same it gives rise to further paradoxes. On the other hand, if we accept that the theory of Aryan invasion is a myth, that there was in fact no such invasion as the proponents and supporters of the theory claim, and that the chronology of Vedic events as arbitrarily fixed by Max Müller was wrong, as was accepted and admitted by BBC and recanted subsequently for obvious reasons, the paradoxes as shown and set out hereinabove automatically disappear and do not survive.

Let us now examine the allegations, observations, comments and rhetoric of Mr Amartya Sen on the so-called rewriting of Indian history by the Hindutva champions which was entirely based on the acceptance of Aryan invasion theory of India and chronology of Vedic literature as formulated by Max Müller, as established facts. Mr Sen says that the "Indus Valley civilization," dating from the third millennium BCE, flourished well before the timing of the earliest Hindu literature, the Vedas, which are typically dated in the middle of the second millennium BCE. As pointed out above, he however does not give any proof or evidence for his soconfident assertion in spite of all the astronomical, ecological and literary evidence to the contrary. Having arbitrarily, and on the basis of speculative philological evidence as shown above, determined the date of composition of the *Rigveda*, the proponents of the theory and its supporters interpreted the *Rigveda* taking the said date as the basis, and the result was devastating and riddled with paradoxes. In order to find out the age and the place of a thing especially literature like *Rigveda*, language cannot be the only criterion. One will have to go through and read the book to find out if any clue is available before coming to any conclusion. Moreover one should never give goodbye to logic and common sense by giving full scope to the imagination to rule as is being done in case of *Rigveda*. In *Rigveda* itself there are many clues on the basis of which one can easily find out its age and the place if only one studies it impartially and without any preconceived ideas or notions.

One such clue is the description of river Sarasvati, another is the word *samudra,* which I have already dealt with while discussing the paradoxes, created by the theory of Aryan invasion. Yet another clue is the astronomical statements appearing in the *Rigveda* about the positions of the stars, the first day of spring (vernal equinox) and the Sun entering the constellation of Krittika (Pleiades in Taurus) on the basis of which Lokmanya Tilak in 1893 determined the age of *Rigveda* as not later than 4000 BCE (*The Orion by Lokmanya Bal Gangadhar Tilak*, 5th edn., 1972), which supports the description of the river Sarasvati as appearing in *Rigveda,* since in 4000 BCE the river Sarasvati was flowing in full force and vigour.

Mr Sen has accused and charged the Hindutva champions of attempting to rewrite Indian history by making the Sanskrit-speaking composers of the Vedas also the same people who created the Indus Valley civilization. No Mr Sen, the Hindutva champions are not attempting to rewrite Indian history through the simple device of "making" the Sanskrit-speaking composers of the Vedas also the same people who created the Indus Valley civilization as alleged by you to remove their difficulties as stated by you and set out by me earlier. In fact, these difficulties have cropped up only because of the acceptance as established facts of the half-baked theory of Aryan invasion and of the arbitrary fixing of the chronology of the Vedic literature without proper evidence. What the Hindutva champions are saying is that since the supporters of the theory, in spite of passing of more than a century, cannot remove the anomalies and defects and explain satisfactorily the paradoxes — as pointed out above, to the theory which have appeared only after the acceptance of the theory as established fact, and on the other hand, whatever new evidences that have found or discovered, do not support the theory — the theory should not be accepted as established fact until the supporters of the theory prove it beyond doubt, and till then the history, as was understood before the rewriting of the history of India by the proponents and supporters of the Aryan invasion theory on the basis of that theory, should be restored. What they are doing is, restoring the history in its original form.

As regards Indus Valley civilization, it was renamed "Indus-Sarasvati civilization," not in honour of a non-observable river called the Sarasvati which is referred to in Vedas as alleged by Mr Sen, but because of the fact that the said civilization was formed and established and was in existence on the banks of the river Sarasvati when it was flowing with full force and vigour before drying up. Only because it has now dried up and is no more in existence and is non-observable you cannot say that it is not "Indus-Sarasvati civilization."

Next we will consider Mr Sen's remarks about a second challenge, which relates to the arrival of the Indo-Europeans (sometimes called Aryans) from the West, most likely in the second millennium BCE, riding horses (unknown in the Indus Valley civilization), as also about concocted Vedic science and Vedic mathematics and alleged marshalling of the "new" archaeological evidence which is a very serious charge and which appears to have been made lightly without proper study of the records available or by ignoring the same.

10

The Reasons for Rejecting the Theory

AMARTYA SEN speaks about the arrival of the Indo-Europeans (sometimes called Aryans) from the West, most likely in the second millennium BCE, riding horses (*unknown in the Indus Valley civilization*). He also charges Natwar Jha and N.S. Rajaram for producing in their book *The Deciphered Indus Script*, published in 2000, a picture of terracotta seal with a horse on it, which was meant to be further proof of the Vedic- and Aryan-identity of the Indus civilization, which he says, is the result of a simple fraud based on a computerized distortion of a broken seal of a unicorn bull which was known earlier, on the authority of a joint essay written by Michael Witzel, professor of Sanskrit at Harvard University, with Steve Farmer, not only criticizing Jha and Rajaram, but also charging them that they, in their book, had fabricated the images of a horse in order to show that the Harappan civilization was Vedic, without in any way giving any proof or evidence for levelling such a serious charge. He it appears insists that any data that suggests otherwise or contrary to his views must perforce be a fabrication. This is what N.D. Kazanas, *In RV Data — A postscript* (Revision A, 23rd May 2001) has to say on the translation of *Baudhayana Srautrasutra* by Witzel: "It did not occur to me that so eminent a Sanskritist would be mistranslating." Witzel also asserts that while Vedas are full of references to horses, the Indus remains with no horses.

While Witzel has charged Jha and Rajaram of fabricating the image of horse, Sen has gone a step further by making a serious allegation, without of course giving any proof or evidence whatsoever, that the alleged horse seal was a distinct product of the late twentieth century, and *the credit for the creation of which has to go to the Hindutva activists*. Even assuming that the horse seal was a computerized distortion of a broken seal of a unicorn bull as alleged by him, how can a person of his stature, assume and allege that the credit for its creation goes to the Hindutva activists without giving any proof whatsoever for making such an allegation. I can only say that such an attitude especially on the part of a person like Mr Sen is highly deplorable and only shows his bias against Hindutva. As regards the alleged computerized distortion of a broken seal of a unicorn bull, the same could have been verified from the actual seal. But the question is not of one seal. That is one of the proofs given by them. In the book *Vedic Aryans and the Origins of Civilization* by N. S. Rajaram and David Frawley, they have given a photo of another pre-Harappan artefact, which also relates it to the *Rigveda*, and that is the photo of a vase from Mehrgarh dated to 4500 BCE. It carries the image of a "winged horse," a composite animal described in the *Rigveda*. It also carries depictions of the *asvattha* leaf, which is considered sacred in the *Rigveda*. And if someone again wants to call it as a computerized distortion, one can verify the fact from the artefact itself. Apart from the above evidence, this is what S.R. Rao one of the world's foremost authorities on Indus archaeology has to say on the point:

> The negative evidence in the form of absence of the horse and rice in the Indus civilization which was taken as evidence of its Dravidian origin is no more tenable in view of the occurrence of the horse bones and rice at Lothal, Kalibangan, Surkotada and Ropar in India and Mohenjo-Daro in Pakistan.

> On the other hand, there is enough positive evidence in support of the religious rites of the Harappans being similar to those of the Vedic Aryans. Their religious motifs, deities and sacrificial altars bespeak of Aryan faith . . . .

One of the major contributions made by the Harappans is *yoga* which the Vedic Aryans also practised. Several terracotta figures of Harappa are depicted in yogic *asana*s. (Talageri 1993: p. vii)

Further excavations have discovered horses not only in Harappan but also in pre-Harappan sites.

The discovery of bones of Equus caballus Linn (the true horse) from so many Harappan sites *and that too right from the lowest levels clearly establishes that the true domesticated horse was very much in use.* (A.K. Sharma, "The Harappan Horse Was Buried Under The Dunes," *Puratattva* 23)

Moreover the encyclopaedia *The Dawn of Indian Civilization*, vol. 1, Part 1 (pp. 344-45) observes: "The horse was widely domesticated and used in India during the third millennium BCE over most of the area covered by the Indus-Sarasvati (or Harappan) Civilization."

Sir John Marshall, Director General of the Archaeological Survey when Harappa and Mohenjo-Daro was being excavated, recorded the presence of what he called "the Mohenjo-Daro horse." Giving salient measurement, comparing it to the other known specimen, he wrote: "It will be seen that there is a considerable degree of similarity between these various examples, and it is probable the Anau horse, the Mohenjo-Daro horse and the example of Equus Caballus of the Zoological Survey of India, are all of the type of the "Indian country bred," a small breed of horse, the Anau horse being slightly smaller than the others." (*Mohenjo-Daro and the Indus*

Civilization, vol. II, p. 654). In verse 1.162.18, the *Rigveda* describes the horse as having 34 ribs (17 pairs) while the Central Asian horse has 18 pairs (36) of ribs. This means that the horse described in the Vedas is the native Indian breed (with 34 ribs) and not the Central Asian variety. Fossil remains of Equus Sivalensis (the Siwalic horse) shows that the 34-ribbed horse has been known in India going back tens of thousands of years. (From an article by N.S. Rajaram that appeared in *The Hindu* on 19 February, 2002). Of course, Witzel has challenged the findings of Marshall saying *inter alia* that the bones of horses found in the excavation do not come from secure level without giving any proof for his conclusions. Mr R. Nagaswamy, Director of Archaeology in Tamil Nadu has in his article in *The Hindu* has refuted systematically Witzel's claim and method calling the latter an example of *reductio ad absurdum*.

K.D. Sethna, the *pitamaha* of the Indian historians, proves conclusively, on the evidence of the use of cotton in north-west India, that the *Rigveda* preceded the Harappan Culture in the Indus Valley. (*Indian Science and Technology in the Eighteenth-Century,* Impex India, Delhi 1971).

"The *Rigveda* no less than the Harappa culture, flourished in the Indus Valley." "None of the three Vedas, none of the numerous Brahmanas and Aranyakas, none of the early principal Upanishads contain the word *karpasa* (cotton).

"The Vedic literature from the *Rigveda* down to the *sutra* period contains numerous references to weavers, the art of weaving, the weaver's shuttle, weaving of clothes like turbans, shirts, etc. soiled garments and washermen.

"The texts also contain very frequent reference to wool (*samulya* and *urna*) and to a cloth made from the bark of the *tripa* or *triparna* tree. Cotton (*karpasa*) is mentioned for the first time in the earliest *sutras*, and silk (*kauseya*) is mentioned for the first time in the *Vasistha Dharmasutra*, which is considered to be a rather late *sutra*. Archaeologically, cotton is first attested in the Indus sites around 2500 BCE. This proves that the age of the four Vedas, the Brahmanas and Aranyakas and the early principal Upanishads preceded the age of the Indus culture." (Shrikant G. Talageri, *Aryan Invasion and Indian Nationalism*, Voice of India, 1993).

From the above evidence it will be quite clear that the Vedic literature especially the *Rigveda* was composed much before the Indus civilization. But the so-called eminent historians are so dogmatic that they are not ready to consider or accept such proofs. They insist that linguistic evidence supersedes all other evidence as if philological evidence is the only evidence in such cases to be considered even though it may be a speculative one, illogical and leads to absurdity. They forget that a historical theory must account for all the evidence and not selectively accept and ignore data, and that a man-made theory cannot substitute for primary data.

Mr Sen alleges that in order to remove the difficulties faced by Hindutva champions, they are rewriting Indian history making the Sanskrit-speaking composers of the Vedas also the very same people who created the Indus Valley civilization, but he never produces a single evidence to the contrary in support of his claims, nor does he disprove the above evidence produced against the theory of invasion. He does not say anything as to how and when these difficulties of Hindutva champions surfaced for the first time, for otherwise he will be faced with the difficult problem of explaining why such difficulties arose at all. These difficulties along with the paradoxes pointed out earlier started from the nineteenth century when history of India, rewritten on the basis of a theory — the theory of Aryan invasion of India — propounded by Max Müller and others as also on the basis of the chronology of Vedic literature fixed by them arbitrarily, was accepted as established fact in spite of all the contrary evidence found and discovered. It will be pertinent to note that there was neither any difficulty nor any paradox earlier to the acceptance of the theory. Mr Sen says that the problem with this account is, of course, its obvious falsity, going against all the available evidence based on archaeology and literature and in the footnote clarifies that we have to distinguish between three distinct errors that are conflated together in this invented history, of course, by the Hindutva champions, and not by the proponents of the Aryan invasion theory. He, however, even though says and claims that it is based on archeological and literary evidence, as usual, does not give even one such proof or evidence in support of his assertion. No doubt, the errors, as pointed out by him have arisen because of the theory — but not any theory invented by the Hindutva champions as assumed by him — of the Aryan invasion invented by its proponents without any evidence — archaeological, literary or otherwise. Naturally, all the errors and difficulties as pointed out by him, as also the paradoxes indicated above will automatically disappear if the invasion theory is rejected.

Before concluding, it is necessary to clarify one more point raised by Mr Sen. He says that the Hindutva enthusiasts have been great champions of so-called Vedic mathematics and Vedic science allegedly developed in splendid isolation in exceedingly ancient India, and as it happened there is no sophisticated mathematics in Vedas nor anything that can be called rigorous science. There were, however, much of both in India in the first millennium CE (after the Greek and Babylonial contributions).

But who have claimed that there is sophisticated mathematics or rigorous science in Vedas as alleged by him? Nobody has said that the Vedas contain sophisticated mathematics or rigorous science. What is being said is that post-Vedic or late Vedic text or literature contains Vedic mathematics, better known as *Sulbasutras*, and the contention that *Sulbasutras* is of earlier origin than that of Egypt and Old-Babylonia is not by any of the Hindutva champions but by the late A. Seidenberg, the distinguished American mathematician and historian of science who traced the unique origin of mathematics to a class of late Vedic texts called *Sulbasutras*. The Sulbas are part of the early Sutra literature, which followed upon the final redaction of the Vedas.

These *Sulbasutras* (or *Sulvasutras*), often referred to as the Sulba, are extremely interesting works that shed a good deal of light cn the early history of mathematics. A comparison of the Sulba of Baudhayana, Apastamba and Katyayana, with the mathematics of Old-Babylonia and Egypt enables us to establish 2000 BCE as the absolute lower limit for the early *sutra* literature. Supplementing this with the astronomical data from the *Asvalayana Grhyasutra*, the *Sathapatha Brahmana* and other works allow us to push this date back by another thousand years. As a consequence, the traditional date for the Mahabharata War (3102 BCE) also becomes supportable (*Vedic Aryans and the Origins of Civilization*, N.S. Rajaram and David Frawley, Voice of India, pp. 138-39).

Late A. Seidenberg, made a close study of the connections between the mathematics — specially geometry — of the Pythagorean Greeks, Old-Babylonia, Egypt and the *Sulbasutras*, and established that all three derive from a common single source He summarized the relationship as follows:

1. *A common source for the Pythagorean and Vedic mathematics is to be sought either in the Vedic mathematics or in an older mathematics very much like it.*
2. The view that Vedic mathematics is a derivative of Old-Babylonia having been rejected, a common source of these mathematics, different from Old-Babylonia of 1700 BCE was indicated.
3. Thus what are regarded as the two main sources of Western mathematics, namely Pythagorean mathematics and Old-Babylonian mathematics, *both flow from a still older source* (Seidenberg 1978: p. 329).

From the above one thing is clear that the Vedic mathematics has not come after the Greek and Babylonian contributions as indicated by Mr Sen. In fact, anyone with simple common sense must have found that the architectural structures of the Harappans, which are of pre-Old-Babylonian period, could not have been built without the knowledge of geometry. But the question is, what is this still older source Seidenberg is speaking about, from which Pythagorean and Old-Babylonian mathematics have flown? Seidenberg himself has provided the answer. He says: ". . . its mathematics was very much like what we see in the *Sulvasutra*s. In the first place, it was associated with ritual. Second there was no dichotomy between number and magnitude: . . . In geometry it knew the Theorem of Pythagoras and how to convert a rectangle into a square. It knew the isosceles trapezoid and how to compute its area. It had a facility with whole numbers and knew some number theory centred on the existence of Pythagorean triples. It had a canonical solution for the circulature of the square: and in its attempts to square the circle, it learned to compute a square root." (Seidenberg 1978: p. 329)

Even though the description of the source given by Seidenberg fits in Sulba itself, why did he not treat Sulba as the source? The answer appears to be because his findings, or at least the implications of it, met with immediate resistance from a few Sanskrit scholars he seems to have consulted as noted by him: "Sanskrit scholars do not give me a date so far back as 1700 BCE (for the *Sulbasutras*). Therefore I postulate a pre-Old-Babylonian source for the kind of geometric rituals we see preserved in the *Sulbasutras*, or at least for the mathematics involved in these rituals." (Sidenberg 1978: p. 329)

Further, for the Indians geometry is primary, while with the Egyptians and Babylonians it is secondary as also in India geometry is secondary to religion and rituals, while in Babylonia and Egypt religious roots are nowhere to be seen. And this gives the reason why the Sulba must have been the source of Old-Babylonian and Egyptian mathematics. The Indians have geometric algebra, and the roots of it are found only in the Sulba. Just as the mathematics of Old-Babylonia cannot be the source for Pythagorean Greece, neither it is possible to derive the geometric algebra of the Sulba from it. As Seidenberg observes:

"Whatever the difficulties there may be (concerning chronology) it is small in comparison with the difficulty of deriving the Vedic ritual application of the theorem from Babylonia . . . further the application involves geometric algebra, and there is no evidence of geometric algebra from Babylonia. And the geometry of Babylonia is always secondary whereas in India it is primary. Hence we do not hesitate to place the Vedic rituals, or more exactly, rituals exactly like them, far back of 1700 BCE." (Seidenberg 1962: p. 515)

It will now be quite clear, that there was never any Aryan invasion of India and that the chronology of Vedic literature fixed by Max Müller and others was not correct. In the circumstances the allegations, charges and contentions of Mr Sen against the Hindus, Hindutva and Hindutva champions made on the basis of Aryan invasion theory and the chronology of Vedic literature, do not stand. Anyone who is interested to know more, may refer to the following books, viz. (1) *Aryan Invasion Theory and Indian Nationalism*, Shrikant G. Talageri, Voice of India, New Delhi; (2) *Vedic Aryans and the Origin of Civilization*, Navaratna S. Rajaram and David Frawley, Voice of India, New Delhi; and (3) *Gods, Sages and Kings — Vedic Secrets of Ancient Civilization*, David Frawley, Motilal Banarsidass Publishers Pvt. Ltd., Delhi.

11

Sen's Analysis for BJP's Failure in 2004 Elections Considered

BEFORE concluding, it is necessary to examine the analysis made by Mr Sen of the situation as to BJP failure in the 2004 election, and the conclusion arrived at by him. Unluckily, it appears from his writings that he has not made an impartial and rational analysis of the situation. What it reveals is his partisan and bias attitude especially against Hindutva while arriving at the conclusions. For everything he blames Hindutva alleging that the Hindutva movement has entered into a confrontation with the idea of India itself and that this is nothing short of a sustained effort to miniaturize the broad idea of a large India and to replace it by the stamp of a small India, bundled around a drastically downsized version of Hinduism. Such a one-sided and biased attitude in analysing the situation will not help for the National Integration of India, which is the main motive of our Constitution. It will only disintegrate and divide India and polarize the communities further. If the intention is to discredit Hinduism in the name of Hindutva movement in the eyes of his readers, it will succeed only with those who are not familiar and are not aware of what is Hinduism and how the political parties are trying to divide India on the basis of religion, caste, creed, sect, class, etc. only in order to gain short-term political advantage. Unfortunately for India, nowadays there are many Indians who profess to be Hindus, and though highly educated (in fact, literate) are not aware of what Hinduism is or what are its principles. They have, in their life, not read any Hindu religious or philosophical books, not even *Gita*. Their Hinduism is restricted to praying to Hindu gods and sometimes visiting Hindu temples or religious places. Such persons are carried away by propaganda made in the media, especially English, and by such books against Hinduism.

Mr Sen says that despite the veritable flood of religious practices in India, there is a resilient undercurrent of conviction that religious beliefs, though personally significant, are socially unimportant and should be politically inconsequential. Ignoring the importance of this underlying conviction has the effect of systematically overestimating the role of religion in Indian society. What he speaks about conviction may be correct so far as intellectuals are concerned. But not with common persons, especially of religious minorities, who are moreover mostly illiterate. In India, for religious minorities, religion occupies a prominent place in their life both personally and socially as well as politically. And that is the reason why our politicians are trying to pamper and appease them for getting their votes.

Mr Sen in the footnote states that the Indian understanding of secularism, which has emerged mainly from its history of tolerant pluralism, is inclined towards favouring neutrality of the state between members of different religious communities. This is complete distortion of the actual facts. The Indian understanding of secularism is not the same, as it is being understood in the West. Favouring neutrality of the state between members of different religious communities is the understanding of secularism in the West and not in India where secularism means favouring the religious minorities maybe for obtaining their votes. Leave aside passing of Acts by the Indian Parliament like Haj Act, but even under the Indian

Constitution, some additional rights are bestowed on the minorities because of which some Hindu sects such as Ramakrishna Mission and Jains were tempted to claim minority status for claiming the benefits enjoyed by minorities. In India while the government is very particular not to interfere with the religion and personal laws of minorities, it interferes with the religion, *ashrams* and Mutts and personal laws of the religious majority with impunity. In fact, what is being practised in India in the name of secularism, is minorityism. And Mr Sen speaks about neutrality of the Indian state!

Mr Sen's analysis of BJP's defeat or debacle in the elections held in 2002, 2003 and 2004 is also far from reality. For the purpose of analysing, he distinguishes between (1) evident societal tensions that may be seen between pugnacious spokesmen of communities identified by different religious ancestries and (2) actual religious tensions in which the contents of religious beliefs are themselves material. He says that the enthusiasts for religious politics have mainly worked through generating societal frictions in which the demographic correlates of religion have been used to separate out the communities for selective roguery (as happened, to a great extent, in Gujarat in 2002). He continues that in this, the finery of religious beliefs has typically played little or no part. He further wants us to appreciate the distinction between religious strifes, and political discords based on utilizing communal demography. He says that the use of militant "Hindutva" may have worked well in the state elections in December 2002 in strife-torn Gujarat, with whipped up hysteria. But as the delirium quietened, the excitement of Hindutva activism delivered very little to sectarian politics in the four state elections held a few months later, in February 2003.

He forgets that in such a type of riots as happened in Gujarat 2002, the finery of religious beliefs hardly plays any part. Why there was genocide of Sikhs in 1984 after the murder of Mrs Indira Gandhi? Why there was a riot in Mumbai in 1993 after the demolition of the so-called Babri Masjid? Why there were riots all over India after the murder of Mahatma Gandhi in 1948 attacking brahmins? What part the finery of religious beliefs has played in these cases? Such riots take place as a sort of reaction or revenge to an earlier action and it is directed against the community or class, which is responsible for the earlier action. As regards Gujarat riots, one should never forget that it happened only because of the horrid act of Muslims, in roasting alive the commuters of a railway bogey at Godhra. One should not try to isolate the riots in Gujarat in 2002 from the earlier incident of Godhra as is being done. It should be remembered that had there been no Godhra incident, there would never have been any riots in Gujarat in 2002. So also the contention of Mr Sen that the use of militant "Hindutva" may have worked well in the state elections in December 2002 in strife-torn Gujarat is not correct and far from reality. In Gujarat there was temporary polarization amongst Hindus mainly because of the biased and one-sided reporting by the English and electronic media.

Mr Sen's analysis of the debacle of BJP in elections held in February 2003, November 2003 and in May 2004 is peculiar, to say the least. He says that the defeat of BJP in the four states including Himachal Pradesh in the elections held in February 2003 is due to the quietening of the delirium caused by the use of militant Hinduism in Gujarat elections in December 2002 because of which the excitement of Hindutva activism delivered very little to sectarian politics, while the success in winning at the polls in three out of four state elections held in November 2003 is because of shifting the focus of its campaign by BJP to developmental issues, with religious demography taking a back seat. Again BJP suffered in 2004 general election because the issue of divisiveness surfaced again as also because of its cultivation of sectarianism and targeting of minorities making it look like a very divisive force in India. In short, except for the Gujarat elections of 2002 where the use of militant "Hindutva" has worked, at other places where BJP has won it is because of its focusing on developmental issues, and where it has failed it is because of its following Hindutva principles of sectarianism and targeting minorities and undermining of a secular India. He, of course, is aware of the hollowness of his arguments and that is why he explains further saying that any set of election results, especially like in India would tend to carry the impact of many different types of influences. But, he says that looking to the nature of the electoral reverses of the BJP and its allies in the elections, including near-total demise of the "secular" parties in alliance with the BJP, it is difficult to miss a general sense of grievance about the neglect of secular concerns by parties which were not formally signed up for the Hindutva agenda. He ignores that BJP suffered mainly because of its reverses in Tamil Nadu and Andhra Pradesh. In Tamil Nadu it has in fact left its earlier partner DMK, which was also a partner in the government, to join hands with AIADMK who had defeated DMK in the state elections, held earlier. While in Andhra Pradesh where state elections were also held along with the general elections, BJP as also Naidu suffered badly because of the Telangana agitation. And it is mainly because of the reverses in Tamil Nadu and Andhra Pradesh that BJP suffered. If as analysed by Mr Sen, BJP and its alliance's reverses in the general elections were due to the neglect of secular concerns by parties, then how would he explain the defeat of RJD of Laloo Prasad and Congress, both supposed to be core secular parties, in the recent state elections held in Bihar?

As regards "soft Hinduism," Mr Sen explains that in responding to the exploitation of religious demography in the politics of Hindutva, the defenders of secular politics often take for granted that the Indian population would want religious politics in one form or another, which has led to the political temptation to use "soft Hindutva" as a compromise response by secularists to the politics of "hard Hindutva." What an explanation? The question is, when did it dawn on these secularists that the Indian population would want religious politics in one form or another and to go for "soft Hindutva" as a response to the politics of "hard Hindutva?" Surely not during the first 50 years or so after Independence. They remembered of the same for the first time only during the Gujarat elections in 2002 December, when there was temporary polarization between the two communities. However much Mr Sen and others may try to explain the "soft Hindutva" adopted by these secularists during Gujarat elections, the fact remains, as exposed in the Gujarat elections of 2002, that their secularism is by way of strategy to obtain minority votes which in India are always polarized, and not as a principle, and the moment they will find that the Hindus in India are getting polarized, they will be the first to adopt "soft Hindutva, not hard Hindutva" to woo Hindus. Only because it did not help them and they could not get any dividend in that election, Mr Sen says that such an approach is foundationally mistaken.

Lastly let us consider his analysis of "small India" and "large India." He speaks about Rabindranath Tagore's idea that the "idea of India" itself militates against the intense consciousness of the separateness of one's own people from others. He says that through their attempt to encourage and exploit separatism, the Hindutva movement has entered into a confrontation with the idea of India itself. And this is nothing short of a sustained effort to miniaturize the broad idea of a large India — proud of its heterodox past and its pluralist present — and to replace it by the stamp of a small India bundled around a drastically downsized version of Hinduism, and that cognizance of India's past is important for an adequate understanding of the capacious idea of India. But, even assuming that what he says about the Hindutva movement is correct, has he ever thought of analysing why the Hindutva movement only now, and not in the past, has entered into a confrontation with the idea of India itself through its attempt to encourage and exploit separatism? Was it not his sacred duty, as a patriotic Indian intellectual who is interested in National Integration of India, to analyse and find out the reasons for the Hindutva movement to encourage and exploit separatism as alleged by him, only now and not in the past? It was surely not difficult for him to find out the reasons had he tried sincerely, but the results may not have been palatable to him and that may be the reason why he did not even attempt to analyse the problem.

However, before analysing the problem, it is necessary to see and examine the principles of the three main religions in India, viz. Hinduism, Islam and Christianity, Hinduism being the main and ancient religion. As admitted by Mr Sen, while Hindu religion is a liberal and tolerant religion, because of which there is the tradition of peaceful presence of different faiths, side by side in India. The same cannot be said about the other two religions. Both are intolerant to other religions even though in the present era they cannot help and have to tolerate other religions. And that is the reason why there were religious wars, *jihads*, crusades and inquisitions in the past. But even though there are no religious wars nowadays, they are indulging in conversions — conversions of people from other religions especially Hindus, to their religion — in a very systematic way, thus causing tension between religions. Secondly, while these religions, viz. Islam and Christianity are a sort of compact religions, in the sense that their religious heads and authorities play important part in the lives of their followers, the same is not the case with Hindu religion. In the Hindu religion, religious authorities hardly play any part in the lives of its followers. Taking the above factors into consideration, let us analyse the situation.

Even though India has adopted a secular constitution, it is secularism with a difference. While all over the world there are minority religious communities in the states, which are secular, there is no country other than India, which has bestowed special rights under the constitution on the religious minority communities in the name of secularism. Further, India is a unique country where the religious duty cast on the followers of a religion — to propagate the religion — is considered a constitutional right with the result that the so-called secularists claim that when a follower of such a religion propagates his or her religion and converts the people from another religion (Hindu) to his or her religion he or she does so in fulfilment of the constitutional right. Moreover while the percentage of minority community (Hindus) in our neighbouring countries is dwindling year by year, in India it is steadily increasing (especially Muslims) not only due to births in the communities but also due to systematic conversions through well-organized machineries such as Christian missionaries. In addition, there are separate minority commissions appointed by states to look after and protect the interests of religious minorities, even though there is a Human Rights Commission already functioning. For the majority religion there is no such commission — Majority Commission — appointed to protect their rights that are being violated not only by religious minority communities, but also by government by interfering not only in their personal laws but also in their religious institutions. The only institution that speaks on their behalf is the Sangh Parivar, which is branded and ridiculed by Mr Sen and other so-called secularists as communal. Even though the modern historians, as also (now) the BBC website, are all agreed that the Aryan invasion of India was a myth and the arbitrary fixing of chronology of Vedic literature as also the history rewritten on the basis of Aryan invasion was wrong, Mr Sen and his renowned Marxist historians are still clinging to the defunct theory of Aryan invasion and the chronology of Vedic literature arbitrarily fixed by Max Müller and others, alleging and charging the Hindutva champions of rewriting the history, to suit the so-called prejudices of Hindutva. Even though the religious minority communities not only *attempt* to encourage and exploit but also *actually* encourage and exploit separatism, the Hindutva movement is charged with the effort to miniaturize the broad idea of a large India and forgetting tolerance and giving belligerently sectarian interpretation to Hinduism. How does Mr Sen expect the Hindus to act in the face of such onslaught on Hinduism? To keep quiet and ultimately to see the wiping out of Hinduism from the earth — a feat that could not be accomplished even by the barbarous invaders, is now being completed by the religious minorities with the help of the so-called secularists and persons like Mr Sen?

Mr Sen's book *The Argumentative Indian* may have been read and appreciated by many and may have been translated in many languages, but it does not give a correct picture and the biased and one-sided views expressed therein will surely not help India in its aim of national integration; on the other hand it will polarize the religious communities and ultimately disintegrate India further.

Bibliography

Aiyar, Mani Shankar, *Confession of a Secular Fundamentalist*, New Delhi: Viking Penguin Group, 2004.

Danino, Michel, *Is Indian Culture Obsolete?*, Mysore: the Mother's Institute of Research and Mira Aditi, 2000.

Danino, Michel and Sujata Nahar, *The Invasion that Never Was*, Mysore: Mother's Institute of Research and Mira Aditi, 2000.

Elst, Koenread, *The Demographic Siege*, New Delhi: Voice of India, 1998.

Frawley, David, *The Myth of Aryan Invasion of India*, New Delhi: Voice of India, 1994.

——, *The Rig Veda*, New Delhi: Aditya Prakashan, 2001.

———, *Hinduism*, New Delhi: Voice of India, 1995.

———, *Hinduism and The Clash of Civilization*, New Delhi: Voice of India, 2002.

———, *From The River of Heaven*, New Delhi: Motilal Banarasidass, 1992.

Frawley, David and N.S. Rajaram, *Vedic Aryans and The Origin of Civilization*, New Delhi: Voice of India, 2001.

Huntington, Samuel P., *The Clash of Civilization and Remaking of World Order*, New Delhi: Penguin Books 1997.

James, Venderkam and Peter Flint, *Dead Sea Scrolls*, New York: Harper Collins Publishers, 2002.

Narain, Harsh, *Myth of Composite Culture and Equality of Religion*, New Delhi: Voice of India, 1997.

Paliwal, K.V., *Max Müller*, New Delhi: Hindu Writer's Forum, 2006"

Radhakrishnan, S., *Eastern Religion and Western Thought*, New Delhi: Oxford University Press, 2006.

———, *The Idealist View of Life*, London: Unusin Paperbacks, 1980.

———, *Recovery of Faith*, New Delhi: Hind Pocket Books (P) Ltd., 1968.

———, *Religion and Culture*, New Delhi: Hind Pocket Books (P) Ltd., 1968.

Sardesai, V.S., *Somanatha by Romila Thapar*, A Critical Study, Mumbai: Hindu Voice, 2005.

———, *Can a Secular be a Fundamentalist?*, Mumbai: Hindu Voice, 2005.

Sen, Amartya, *The Argumentative Indian*, Great Britain: Allen Lane, 2005.

———, *Identity and Violence*, Great Britain: Allen Lane, 2006

Shaikh, Anwar, *The Vedic Civilization*, United Kingdom: Principality Publisher 2003.

Shourie, Arun, *Eminent Historians*, New Delhi: ASA 1998.

Talageri, Shrikant G., *Aryan Invasion Theory and Indian Nationalism*, New Delhi: Voice of India, 1993.

Thapar, Romila, *Somanatha*, New Delhi: Viking Penguin, 2004.

———, *Early India*, New Delhi: Penguin 2002.

Tilak, Lokamanya Bal Gangadhar, *The Orion*, Pune: J.S. Tilak, 1972.

Index